Bleeding Bull

Published by Red Eye Books, Inc.
Eugene, Oregon 97408

Cataloging-in-Publication Data

Sarkoff, Vladimir.
Bleeding bull : the stock market bubble and the American middle class / Vladimir Sarkoff. -- 1st ed.
p. cm.
LCCN: 2001-132095
ISBN: 0-9705639-2-2

1. Investments, American--Social aspects. 2. Stock exchanges--United States--Social aspects. 3. Middle class--United States. I. Title

HG4910.S37 2002 332.64'2'73
QBI01-200307

Cover photograph by Jose A. Ortega
Cover design by Colman Fockens and Nicole Riggs

Bleeding Bull

The Stock Market Bubble
And
The American Middle Class

Vladimir Sarkoff

Red Eye Books • Eugene Oregon

The flame departed, but from behind it came a Sicilian bull. Although it was made of brass, it gave forth a confused sound—the lament of the man who was trapped in its belly.

—Dante, *Divine Comedy*

Contents

Bleeding Bull

1
Fireworks

It scarcely matters that truth is a fiction; what is important is only that we agree on that fiction, and that its enunciation should simultaneously confer *authority* . . .

—Mikkel Borch-Jacobsen, *Lacan*

In the waning years of the last millennium, fans of the bull market defended their aging rally from "mania" accusations by calling upon Alan Greenspan as star witness for the New Economy.

In June 1998, the Federal Reserve Bank chairman told Congress, "Our economy is still enjoying a virtuous cycle in which, in the context of subdued inflation and generally supportive credit conditions, rising equity values are providing impetus for spending and, in turn, the expansion of output, employment, and productivity-enhancing capital investment."[1]

But Greenspan's "virtuous cycle" was developing structural cracks even as the chairman lauded it. It was more a vicious cycle than a virtuous one. A few months after this speech, the global financial system almost blew itself to bits on a Molotov cocktail of derivatives, Russian debt, and hedge fund hubris.

It said much about the mood of the times that the Federal Reserve's successful rescue of Long-Term Capital Management (LTCM), a massively overblown trading outfit, set the stage for the stock-buying opportunity of a lifetime. In the unreal atmosphere which developed, successfully extinguishing the fires ignited by a high-speed speculative derailment became grounds for a rally of historic proportions.

The prices of S&P 500 stocks were accelerating at three times the rate of their earnings—and five times the speed of the U.S. economy as a whole. For perhaps the first time in history, large numbers of new companies were being seeded on the basis of nothing more than a good sales pitch. All an ambitious twenty-something needed was an idea, a domain name, a few Java programmers, and he could "go public." During the bull's golden days, technology fads came and went faster than you could count then: B2C, B2B, superconductors, "incubators," broadband, and Linux, to name just a few.

Towards the end of 1999, the Federal Reserve flooded the banking system with liquidity due to misguided fears about a possible Y2K crunch. In the stock-buying binge which ensued, margin debt spiked to record levels.

Novice investors were signing on in droves with online brokers to make their "own investment decisions"—just like the professionals! They discovered a certain romantic thrill in throwing caution to the wind and betting their financial future on technology stocks, which towards the end jittered and jumped like amphetamine junkies at the end of a three-day binge.

The stage was set for a speculative disaster.

Measured in relation to the rest of the U.S. economy, the stock market bubble of the 1990s was the biggest investment mania since the Roaring Twenties. In terms of collective effort, levitating the market ranked right up there with sending a man to the moon. The bubble was either a great leap for mankind—or else the whole country was *trippin' out.*

Most investors didn't monitor their positions closely. They didn't evaluate and adjust portfolio risk regularly. They weren't schooled in the discipline of loss-control, which involves entering stop-loss orders, scaling in and out of positions, and ruthlessly cutting losses.

But then, taking losses wasn't something that most investors were familiar with. In the latter stages of the boom, picking stocks with their eyes closed had worked as well as—if not better than—picking them with their eyes open. Failing to employ appropriate risk management strategies didn't hurt most investors—on the contrary, those who bet on a well-run Aggressive Growth mutual fund doubled their money.

Noting the outsized returns to early investors, people became increasingly willing to pony up the ante. Most Americans were working harder than ever for their money—but what were they doing with it? Good chunks of it were going towards rounding up, say, a $40-billion ransom to help one tech behemoth acquire a little brother. Now *that's* what we call public cooperation! Dollars were dutifully dispatched to join the fray.

History will view the rally's final, stubborn, blindly bullish leg, which lifted the Nasdaq Composite Index over 5000, as ironic. Many well-informed investors exited their long positions well below the eventual top, while many less-informed investors continued enjoying fantastic (paper) returns, right until the end.

A lot of experienced players bailed out of their longs on technical grounds as broad market breadth wilted, then watched incredulously as the technical indicators remained pinned in "overbought" territory. They stayed on the sidelines over that final stretch, frustrated but unable to commit money to what they knew was an unsustainable rally.

In the mania which could admit to no excess, market veterans had the distinct sensation of watching truth perish before blithe hyperbole. For months they sat on their cash hoards, grumpily preaching the gospel of "value investing" and griping about how stocks were "insanely overpriced." At the time it sounded like sour grapes over missing part of the Greatest Rally of All Time.

What had happened? In the bizarre climate, backing lousy business ideas had become exceedingly profitable.[2]

Like the climax to a magnificent fireworks display, the final run-up in tech stocks was a full-blown buying panic. Buying panics are associated primarily with shortages of essential commodities such as gasoline; finding it present in the equity markets should have given even the sturdiest of bulls pause. After all, the amount of total outstanding stock is potentially infinite; boards of directors can and do authorize secondary offerings and splits; and entrepreneurs can and do bring new companies to market through the IPO process—as many of them as the market will bear.

By late 1999, the market was flooded with new issues. It was a recipe for disaster—but first the Ultimate New Year's Party, with its toasts to Advanced Decadence.

The mighty top came in March 2000. Many investors had never been through a bear market before.

2
The Sound of Hissing Air

The greatness of this image . . . lies in the fact that it is *purely unreal*, though for every dreamer it possesses an indestructible solidity because it is *also* the dream of others . . .

—Jean-Paul Sartre, *The Family Idiot*

Stocks didn't fall all at once; there was too much incipient bullishness for that. The market didn't crash the way it had in October 1987, although many individual technology stocks crashed, one by one, as if stricken by a plague visiting every household in succession.

A summer rally took place on the assumption that money managers would buy stock voraciously when they returned from their annual holidays. After Labor Day, institutional investors did come back from their vacations, but they weren't in a buying mood.

For the rest of the year, the broader market suffered intermittent, but increasingly debilitating, spasms. The dotcoms, which for years had rocketed skyward on a remarkable trajectory, faded like briefly-glimpsed shooting stars.

As poorly as the large cap Nasdaq 100 index was performing, its spectacular swoon only camouflaged what was happening further down in the speculative ranks: Small capitalization tech stocks were being decimated. Yet even as its multi-trillion dollar edifice crumbled, the Nasdaq recorded its biggest one-day gains in history.

One by one, the darlings of the previously stunning advance fell, but the public didn't lose its enthusiasm for stocks. Each dip was predictably bought, but each with slightly less excitement. A number of the one-day gains were impressive, but the short, sharp, failed rallies merely confirmed the diagnosis: Bear Market.

By autumn, the bull was losing a great deal of blood. Even so, market indexes still leapt 5 percent and more in a single day. Next on the hypesters' lists of prophecies came the annual Christmas rally, which, they insisted, arrived with all the regularity of a Salvation Army Santa Claus. The Christmas rally turned out to be just another bull trap.

The first quarter of 2001 was perfectly abominable for investors; for the first time, there was literally no shelter from the storm but cash. Even the invincible Dow gave up ground. Those waiting for a decent rally to dump their stocks into were trapped by a series of lower highs. "It will rebound" became steadily less of a prediction and steadily more of a hope.

Far from being a field of dreams, the market had become a killing field.

3
Don't Look Now

Every opportunistic tendency in the modern world is motivated, in the final instance, by the will to *belong* to one's own world, to move through it like a fish through water, and it is exactly *this* idea of freedom that is expressed in the American glorification of *unself-consciousness*.

—Massimo De Carolis
Towards a Phenomenology of Opportunism

As the decline accelerated, most investors clung to their portfolio of increasingly tarnished equities; some bought even more stock, convinced that shares had become "undervalued." Others beat a partial retreat by "rotating" out of techs—not to raise cash, mind you, but to buy other stocks which they judged "safer."

Bullish complacency showed up in the market sentiment numbers. Smart traders sold into it.

Like the top story of a collapsing building, the top technology names—one might call them the "sentimental favorites"—such as the optical and networking stocks, which had survived relatively unscathed long after the top, seemed to remain airborne for an impossibly long time before finally giving way.

Investors had ridden the roller coaster all the way up—and now, like faithful companions unable to abandon a dear friend, they rode it all the way back down again. People stayed in the market because they were invested at an emotional level as well as a financial one: They were *committed*.

By March 2001, some financial planners were actually suggesting that their clients not look at their financial statements, so as to spare themselves any unnecessary "psychological distress." The market would bounce back before they had a chance to worry about their losses, so why bother? (First among the Axioms of the Psychology of Denial: Never Look At Your Mutual Fund Statements.)

Between January and May 2001, the Fed slashed interest rates at its fastest clip ever, but the repeated infusions of liquidity were like handing an overly-winded jogger a high-protein energy bar. As interest rates sank, there ensued a veritable binge of home-buying and mortgage-refinancing, all accompanied by guarantees served up by those most obliging of government agencies, Fannie Mae and Freddie Mac, which were expanding their "books" at the speed of notaries in the midst of an Oklahoma land rush.[1]

At the beginning of April, the market put in a bottom which many technical analysts considered something less than climactic. Investors were betting on a quick economic recovery. In the face of continuously rotten corporate earnings, the indexes retraced roughly a third of their decline. By May 2001, the Dow was even flirting with old highs.

But gasoline prices were hitting ten-year highs, and after a long hibernation, *gold*—that fabled harbinger of inflationary doom—briefly leapt higher. Bond traders, too, were nervous. They wondered if the Fed had given up its fight against price inflation in an imprudent rush to reflate the economy. Like an enormous old Cadillac, the U.S. economy revved higher. Alan Greenspan had the pedal to the metal—but could he see anything through that grimy windshield?

4
Front Row Seating

> What is venial as an occasional expedient is reprehensible when carried on as a regular occupation.
>
> —R.H. Tawney

For decades, television shows such as *Meet the Press* have been jumping-boards for politicians wishing to influence public opinion. So, too, rather quickly after they first came on the air, financial cable TV channels became the stomping grounds of touts representing powerful vested interests.

Among the opportunistic ranks of the characters who fluttered in front of the cameras of the business news channels throughout 2000 were grinning sociopathic "investment advisors," who tirelessly advocated "diversification" and unfailingly addressed call-in viewers by their first names; "street-smart" market mavens who chatted with chief executive officers a great deal by telephone; fatherly anchormen—they were the worst—who, with their endlessly banal market platitudes, did a particular disservice to those investors who mistakenly relied on their falsely reassuring words; faintly seductive, girlfriend-like anchorwomen, who embraced the bull market with all the enthusiasm of cheerleaders; and finally, a steady succession of almost preternaturally incisive-looking CEOs—each one a walking ad for the supremacy of the American Way.

Admittedly, the relationship between the lions of industry and their fervent admirers in the mass media sometimes breaks down. The media can't resist occasionally highlighting the scandalous activities of certain companies which step beyond the pale of acceptable business practice, and CEOs occasionally lambast the media for its "bias" in reporting. The parties aren't in bed with one another—at least, not in the vulgar sense of the term. From time to time, big business and media turn on each other, and when they do, it's for the same reason that they usually work together: To enhance their own power and wealth.

The programming schedule of these channels reflects the expedient nature of their undertaking. On weekdays, cable fiefdoms focus on the financial world, but on weeknights and weekends they often switch their tune, and instead of regaling TV audiences with exciting tales of stock market bonanzas, they serve up low-brow slop.

Entertainment gossip focuses on figures like O.J. Simpson and Monica Lewinsky; financial gossip promotes a similarly cult-like fascination with that other luminary of the small screen: Alan Greenspan. During the stock market bubble and for months after it popped, the financial stations played and replayed the same clips of the chairman walking down the same street on his way to a Federal Open Market Committee (FOMC) meeting. While the lenses zoomed in on the dour, grimly-attired central banker, pundits poured over transcripts of the chairman's latest stiffly-fashioned utterances for clues to his "next move." The obsessive surveillance merely disguised the fact that central bankers have little power to affect the market, except in the short term.

Greenspan had indeed attained a dubious modicum of fame: His image was as jealously sought as O.J. Simpson's had once been.

Did it occur to the marketing masterminds of financial tele-journalism that it might actually be a *good* thing to speak truthfully to their audience about the dangerously overblown market conditions which existed? What—*tell it like it is? Wouldn't that cause a financial panic?*

In the late 1990s, the truth about the U.S. stock market was that it was terribly overvalued, as any market-savvy person looking at a long-term chart of price/earnings (P/E) or market capitalization-to-GDP ratios could have easily pointed out. But most investors didn't bother looking at charts. What they wanted to hear was a bull market fantasy—and that's just what they got.

It's whatever sells, man.

During the bubble, the hardest question an intrepid TV reporter asked a CEO was, "Are you comfortable with those earnings projections?" The CEO was either "reasonably comfortable," "comfortable," "quite comfortable," or "very comfortable."

"I'm comfortable," said the grinning CEO (whether he was or not).

On television, complex financial issues were broken down into simple but false choices "in terms the viewer can understand." Everything was doled up in a comfortingly familiar format. The flavor-of-the-minute spin always consisted of a few simplistic stalking-horses ("Will the Fed Cut?").

When one of these histrionic devices resonated emotionally with viewers (i.e., if a lot of people watched the channel, as measured by the ratings), then the "story" was repeated over and over again, like a broken record.

A favorite ploy of these channels during the 1990s was the follow-the-exec-around-on-IPO-day segment. Cameras recorded a friendly-guy-turned-Internet-tycoon's every tremor as he nervously waited for the first day of trading in his company's stock. The camera focused in on the executive's face as he sat at his desk in a happy daze, watching his profitless company's stock price leap higher on a trading monitor. And of course, the channels didn't forget to remind the audience how much the lucky sod was suddenly worth.

Those hoping the stock market would bounce back in 2000 (thereby rescuing their battered portfolios), needed look no further than their own television screens, where bears were practically banned by the financial channels until bearishness finally became "fashionable"—just in time for the bullish reversal that began in early April, 2001.

For (too) many months after the bubble broke, these channels continued donating airtime to the slick salespeople from investment houses who arrived to utter the same worn-out platitudes: "This is a normal correction," "Stocks are now oversold," "The rally will get going when people get back from their vacations," "The rally is coming as soon as people finish their tax-loss selling," "This market is going to rally explosively as soon as the Fed cuts interest rates . . ."

The truth has never sold particularly well on television.

5
Scorched Earth

Then he laughed: "Bear no suspicion in your heart!
I absolve you in advance, while you instruct me
To raze Penestrino to the ground . . ."

—Dante, *Divine Comedy*

By 1996, the conference rooms of venture capitalists (VCs) had literally become dream factories. The VC (whose hubris was exceeded only by the Greek gods of ancient lore) had, apparently, discovered the ultimate road to riches: *The IPO*.

Beneath their unflappable willingness to squeeze every fad for the maximum payout, the VCs faced a perennial challenge: Squeezing themselves through the traditionally narrow IPO "Window of Opportunity." The secret was unloading their "inventory" at gold rush prices before folks discovered that the liquid gold they'd been exuding from their pores wasn't a permanent wellspring of human wealth.

In 1998, a VC with, say, a dozen technology startups in his stable was sitting atop a potential goldmine—but those companies were burning a big hole in his pocket, because running money-losing enterprises costs money. To make things trickier, a VC normally can't unload his shares in the companies he's bred until several months after IPO day. A golden crop was germinating in the VC's entrepreneurial hothouse, yet he was still months (if not years) from getting the last of his little creations to market and cashing out the fortune that awaited him.

By 1998, the party was already wearing on. But Alan—dear old Alan—had arrived with plenty of refreshments, and there was still time for nimble-footed VCs to rake in their royal prizes.

In fact, the best was yet to come.

6
Uh-Oh

Is land in Kansas one-generation land?

—L.E. Willoughby

As the market entered its topping phase, analysts had less than 1 percent of the stocks they covered rated as "sells"—everything else was either a "buy" or a "hold." In the absence of both the insight and the courage necessary to issue "sell" recommendations on stocks, analysts gave even the worst stocks "hold" ratings. When an analyst said "hold," he meant *sell*—every Wall Streeter knew that, of course. Why didn't the analyst just come out and say so, then? Because he needed his *clients*, who took him at face value, to keep holding—holding the *bag*.

During the mania, analysts raised the price targets of stocks based on price action *alone*. If a stock jumped from, say, 50 to 400, the crystal-ball readers simply announced 500 as their next price target. Once the bubble popped, all their forecasts and prognostications proved grossly inaccurate—and no wonder, since they were all based upon the same absurd premise: Continually booming capital markets.

Eventually these same analysts got around to downgrading entire technology sectors at a stroke of their pens—when it was too late for such cautionary moves to do investors much good, of course.

Most "buy" recommendations from "trusted analysts" were little more than naked tout sheets. Perhaps this lack of objectivity can be explained by the frequently cozy relation between analysts and the senior managements of the companies they "analyze." A CEO or CFO is the source of almost every reportorial "scoop" these analysts have ever printed. Corporate insiders hand out privileged pieces of information like trinkets of a monarch's esteem, and they *always* extract a price for their grandiloquence.

What was missing from the analysts' putatively comprehensive analyses was a sense of context in which to evaluate present conditions in the stock market

As the Nasdaq Composite Index leapfrogged 5000 and pushed still higher, most analysts donned oxygen masks and continued issuing bullish recommendations. Equity research departments were countenancing overvaluation *en masse*. If a stock was priced within the P/E range of others within its industry group and performed just a little better, they rated it "Good Value." *There was no point in scaring a client away by suggesting that* all *stocks were outrageously overpriced, was there?*

Some of these touts repeated the same nonsense at 100-point increments for 3000 points on the way down: The "underlying strength" in the economy would see it through, "cash is building," "the American consumer will pull us through."

Numerous technology rockets were in the process of losing 90 percent of their value, yet famous market pundits were still uttering inspiring imprecations, proclaiming (to all who would listen) that these stocks were "attractive at today's reduced prices."

The bargains were lying right there in the street! You just had to pick them up!

All of this was only the old retailer's trick of "discounting" an item after first marking it up.

We should not necessarily conclude that the equity research departments of the security industry's largest companies were as fooled by the mania as the public was. The analyst is only the face the investment bank shows to the public—and it has many faces. The grand houses are like political parties—they have a *platform* which corresponds to the guidance they give their clients (although their proprietary trading arms often bet in the other direction). Since all of the houses routinely enter short market positions either for hedging or speculative purposes, their perma-bullish chatter must be rated as pap for the masses.

"Opportunity" is the broker's favorite word, but opportun*ism* seems his preferred mode of action.

7
Trust

In the gloom, the gold gathers the light against it.

—Ezra Pound

If you are like most people, you have neither the time nor the inclination to make your own investment decisions; the mutual fund industry sprang up to take advantage of this fact. If you select a mutual fund—or, if you prefer, the mutual fund will pick you, through its incessant advertising—you can, after all applicable management fees and expenses are deducted, hope to equal or occasionally even exceed the returns of the benchmark S&P 500 Index.

Congratulations.

To sell mutual funds, advertisers often choose images with powerful emotional resonance. The mainstay? A tired father, taking a moment away from his financial statements to scoop up a flaxen-haired child (who will now be able to attend college because of her daddy's foresight). As if it is criminally negligent for *any* responsible father *not* to be "fully invested"! Having viewed several thousand such ads on TV, investors could be forgiven for thinking of their best-performing mutual fund as a sort of favorite uncle.

By 1999, the gigantic size to which the mutual fund industry had grown was itself a clear indication that things had gotten badly out of joint. Once upon a time, executives had stubbornly clung to their precious voting shares and vigorously repulsed the attentions of unwelcome suitors. By the 1980s, things had changed. To their considerable delight, moguls discovered they could make far more money packaging and marketing equity products to the small investor than they could by growing a company the "old-fashioned" way.

Hype had been promoted to the executive suite.

To this day, the funds industry encourages people to invest based on their "tolerance to risk." Asset managers often offer prospective clients an impressive palate of funds to choose from; Aggressive Growth funds are intended for the most "risk-tolerant" investors.

In order to properly evaluate risk, investors would need to embark upon a lengthy study of the volatilities of each of the investments held in the funds—a difficult task, since most mutual funds are not transparent; managers only periodically disgorge information on their trading activity.

As the rally aged, many investors seemed unaware that high-volatility tech stocks can lose their value in bear markets even faster than they can acquire it in bull markets. By 1999, the "best" mutual funds had been increasing in value every year for longer than most people could remember. That's why these investments *didn't* seem particularly risky at the time. Few people considered that perhaps *no* fund and *no* amount of risk exposure was appropriate, given how expensive stocks had become.

The small investor's strategy was to find the hottest-performing fund and jump right in—a clear sign that stock market returns, not fundamentals, were driving the mania in its final phase. There was a pervasive, and deeply mistaken, notion among investors that simply buying into the "highest-quality" stocks would generate the best returns; nobody seemed to consider the possibility that some of the very funds which performed best in 1999 would perform *worst* a year later.

Asset managers took the virtues of eternal stock ownership for granted, according the First Principle of Expedience: Sugarcoat It. First-time investors were given an easy time of it. They needed only to choose the packaged fund that was "right for them," and, of course, send money. Beyond that, their friendly mutual fund portfolio manager would make all the decisions *for* them, executing a kind of strategy-in-absentia.

Most fund managers stood by the gospel of Fully Invested throughout the decline, even as the market was collapsing; it is, perhaps, slightly more reprehensible that they pretended to objectivity while continuously touting the virtues of staying permanently long.

For a blissfully long time, ignorance of the markets didn't preclude investors from nabbing paper returns of 20, 30, even 200 percent a year—though (as the mutual funds were careful to warn in the fine print) past returns aren't necessarily indicative of future ones.

It was a nifty deal for all parties concerned. But the Eyes Closed approach to attaining millionaire status couldn't succeed eternally.

8
The Provocation

To give currency to his pretensions, to the end that he may, with impunity, gratify his avarice . . .

—Paul-Henri Holbach, *System of Nature*

By 1999, the potential for further bull market advances was already severely circumscribed by a number of factors. Early the following year, supply met demand. As soon as that happened, the bubble burst.

The market peaked at the moment the last True Believer signed on.

By 2000, investors had been seduced by the utopian but ultimately baseless promise of wealth without effort. The articles of faith which were so regularly preached to them must be rated as propaganda designed to keep them in the game. The dissemination of bullish misinformation throughout the population was a form of ideological manipulation, as next we shall see.

Demand had long been accustomed to chasing stock. At first, it was delighted to be offered such "bargains."

Later, it grew horrified . . .

(1) Permanent Prosperity

The New Economy was the reigning motif of the 1990s bull market. According to its defenders, the mighty "click-through" of the computer mouse had ushered in a new phase of history, a period so remarkable that former asset valuation measures were no longer even relevant.[1]

When stock prices began accelerating faster than the earnings which had traditionally buttressed them, analysts—those zealous advocates of market efficiency—were left with no alternative but to announce that *new valuation levels* applied. You see, everything had become "virtualized"—a form of alchemy that justified stock valuations far more extreme than any since the 1920s.

The annals of history illustrate the spuriousness of such claims. Earlier waves of technological innovation, such the railroad or the automobile, had spurred economic booms in their times, but certainly none had ushered in *permanent prosperity*. Yet this is precisely what the bubbletonians were promising.

In the bubble's latter stages, new technological innovations served primarily as grist for the promotional mills of those who made their living by dumping investment products on the public. At the heart of the myth was the Internet, which offered what (at the time) seemed like a highly compelling proposition: The colonization of the personal computer screen as billboard, a whole new digital advertising surface for companies intrepid enough to "establish a presence" on the web. (Boosters didn't bother mentioning that the Internet was also capable of defeating its own utility by creating an impenetrable, buggy, virus-infested informational glut.)

The business models of the dotcoms were often fatally flawed—but in their heyday, no one noticed. Many sites offered free access to all web visitors—everything would stay free as long as users clicked on enough *banner ads!*

When dotcom executives justified their vastly unprofitable customer promotions, they cited the need to obtain market share at any cost—that sounded good. It was just the sort of gritty "grow-or-die" nonsense that investors were dying to hear, but the very fact that these financially-suicidal giveaways were deemed necessary in the first place was clear evidence of the extreme financial precariousness of the endeavors.

Banner ads and "strategic alliances"— those were the twin pillars of the Grand Theory of Internet Advertising. The annoying ads generated a bit of revenue, but the "strategic alliances"—mostly supported by banner ads that, in the event, merely linked one profitless company to the next—weren't exactly the "new dawn of advertising" that dotcom executives were ecstatically proclaiming.

The incessant patter of blithe claims proved effective in pulling new capital from the middle class, however. Americans put down multi-million-dollar bets on businesses backed by nothing more than the promise of revenues from—you guessed it: Banner-ads.

In 2000, banner ad rates crashed. Was that a surprise?

(2) Market Timing Doesn't Work

If we examine the bull-promoting public-relations mechanism in its entirety, we discover an enormous multi-level institution which included the government, several thousand publicly-traded corporations, the securities industry, and the mass media, all of which functioned more or less seamlessly to promote the illusion of "good faith," "trust," "stability," and "economic progress."

With a compliant set of Fed governors, a billion dollars a year in financial-industry advertising, a forest-denuding heap of glossy magazines, and the airways humming with TV shows spouting continual blather about the "information superhighway" and "productivity gains" and "the virtues of long-term investing," you had a darned bullish situation on your hands—at least, until the bubble popped.

Throughout the 1990s, the whole monstrous public-relations effort, the bombardment of the airways by banks, mutual funds, brokers and other institutions conveyed just one message: *Buy and hold.*

In every mania, a few individuals seem chosen, as if by fate itself, to perfectly enunciate the insane *zeitgeist*. Through their tireless punditry, they move markets. During the last bubble, they collectively delivered 100 percent of the Daily Recommended Pabulum on which bulls relied for emotional sustenance.

Since these pundits work for companies that also often make markets in the financial instruments they rattle so enthusiastically about, it can be observed that they showed exceptional opportunism in catching the golden nuggets as they fell from the table, a vocation for which their dual role (in any other business it would be called a conflict of interest) perfectly prepared them.[2]

The telegenic stars were trotted in front of cameras for morale purposes, to keep the troops from mutinying. Beneath their shallow performances one could discern a darker, always unspoken, truth: The masses *must* remain invested in bad times as well as good, that is to say, they must remain invested *all* the time, because otherwise the whole market would crash and the economy would end up in the soup.

These advocates of the buy-and-hold plan insisted that market timing had never been successfully accomplished since the beginning of financial speculation.[3] This claim seemed designed to forestall the obvious inference that if it is possible to time the market, then people *should* pull their money out now and again.

Since the market is going to bounce sooner or later, it would be a terrible mistake to sell stocks while they are temporarily so weak. Chances are, this is the bottom. In fact, investors are scooping up bargains right off the street.

How much portfolio erosion should an investor be prepared to tolerate, then? *Oh, the market might go down,* they blandly acknowledged, *but except for these occasional stumbles, the bull market will extend to infinity.* The "corrections" (even in early 2001, boosters steadfastly refused to call it a "bear market") were mere blips on the chart.

What about novice investors—should they have bought in, say, at January 2000 prices? *Any time would be a good time to buy stock.* How much risk should investors be prepared to tolerate? *That depends on investor tolerance, but stock market corrections can be substantial.* Should people expect that during these "corrections," their portfolios might lose, say, two-thirds of its value—as the Nasdaq did within 12 months of its high? *No one can predict that.*

The message? *One should buy it all, anytime—at any price.* Under the dogma of full investment, investors must let their losses run—indefinitely. (For those who remain resolute through the bad times, fathomless riches will come.)

The core belief of the Cult of Equities is this: Stocks will *always* be worth more in the future than they were in the past.[4] As an external sign that initiates grasp this abiding truth on a practical level, they are required to *send money* to a mutual fund on some sort of "regular," "systematic," or "automatic investing" basis.

Instead of doubting their bullishness in the face of the market cataclysms of 2000-2001, many investors clung even more rigidly to their articles of bullish faith. Were they expressing—or perhaps repressing—their regret for not selling closer to the top, or for not selling at all?

For months after the market topped, the fear of missing the "next bull leg" was so acute that investors jumped back into the fray—over and over again—at the slightest hint of good news. Good news was scarce—but wishful thinking was abundant.

A bull does not stop running when it is merely jabbed with a few sticks; at first, this mild torture only spurs it on to greater efforts.

(3) Average Down

Averaging down into a falling market is a strategy which requires adding to a long position as the stock drops in price (that is to say, adding as one is losing money) thereby obtaining a lower average buy-in price.

Averaging down works only if the stock market *reverses* in the direction anticipated by the investor (otherwise it is called flushing money down the toilet).

At the start of 2000, many people were already overinvested; averaging down put them still deeper into the hole. The "dippies," as they are known, didn't give up easily—although they paid a fearsome price for their persistent devotions to the god of lucre. Convinced that they *had* to buy all dips if they weren't to miss the next "buying opportunity of the decade," dippies unwisely depleted their cash reserves, like faithful *Ronins* hurling themselves against the upper trendlines of indexes in misguided expenditures of excess.

By Labor Day 2000, the philosophy of averaging down had served to create the world's biggest bull trap.

(4) There is Money Sitting on the Sidelines Waiting to Be Invested

Bubble-boosters realized that "sidelined" money had to be drawn into the market if the downward slide was to be reversed. To entice as many fence-sitters as possible to jump back in, bubbletonians made a major public relations effort, announcing, "A pile of money on the sidelines is waiting to be invested."

A lot of money was indeed sitting on the sidelines—smart money, given the dismal investment outlook. In order to draw the money of bearishly-inclined investors back into the market, boosters told them that sidelined investors (just like themselves) were, in fact, bursting with bullishness—a clever tactic, though hardly good advice at the time!

(5) Rotate

At various stages of the decline, the more hyperactive players rotated their money out of one stock sector and into another. At times, this strategy was like climbing to the masthead of a sinking ship. Yet it saved rattled players the psychological pain of exiting the market altogether—which would have entailed accepting the finality of their recent losses.

Wounded bulls needed fresh reasons for *not* liquidating their positions. What could be more comforting than the assurances of silver-tongued mutual fund brokers that client funds had been "rebalanced to account for the recent volatility"?

The favorite destination of scared money was the Dow Jones Industrial Average. There is nothing like a little pulp and paper to soothe the nerves of shell-shocked refugees from the technology sector.

Things had been different during the bubble. Right up to the day the bubble popped, tech stocks had outperformed value stocks, causing a technical divergence that troubled technical analysts. Once it broke, money ran the other way, and it was value's turn to bask in the sun.

By early 2001, the churning had proved only marginally profitable, for the simple reason that, once again, too much money was trying to take refuge under too small an umbrella. The result? *The overvaluation of "value" stocks.*

Yet, as if artificially levitated, the Dow remained buoyant. After the broad market topped, the prestigious but narrow index played the role of the bull's only remaining poster child, its perceived "safe haven" status remaining largely inviolate. By the spring of 2001, however, the blue-chip gorilla could not resist gravity any longer, and it made a precipitous retreat in the direction of 9000. The index bottomed before it suffered a complete technical breakdown, then began a slow but steady climb back through 11,000—its umpteenth journey past that milepost.

All this played out according to the age-old schema: *The Strongest Are The Last To Go.*

For as long as it continues, widespread avoidance behavior is powerful evidence that capitulation has not yet occurred. In a bear market, the failure to go to cash can easily amount to a *failure* to *take losses*.

An investor who merely signs off on his broker's periodic "asset reallocation" suggestions (but does not actually exit the market altogether) is still listening to the enticing chords of the Pied Piper of Easy Money.

(6) The Bottom Is In

Every couple of hundred points or so along the swiftly plunging journey from Nasdaq 5000 down through Nasdaq 2000, one of the Boys clamped a miniature microphone to the lapel of his or her pinstriped suit and told a cable-television reporter that the bottom was already "in" and the bounce was "coming."

This embellishment to bullish theory held that if there ever *had* been a bubble—something that was by no means admitted—the decline in stock prices, together with the decline in margin debt, had "wrung most of the risk out of the market."

In retrospect, one could see that stocks were—or rather, had been—overvalued. But there had been a shakeout. This was actually a healthy thing, because it had separated the wheat from the chaff. Long-term investors needed only grin and bear it a little longer, and the pain would soon be over.

From the assumption that stocks weren't overvalued at the top, it (apparently) followed indubitably that stocks had grown "cheap" once they had lost half their value. Many "formerly overpriced" issues were now "buying opportunities."

In fact, these stocks represented good value only in relation to their recently bloated highs, not in relation to *any* historical valuation measure. What was unclear was why, if these stocks had been "overpriced" at their highs, the analysts had not removed their "buy" ratings on these stocks then.

By late 2000, bulls understandably wished their ordeal to end, so that it would pass like a brief if vivid nightmare from their minds. But how premature they were, to pronounce their troubles over—as if the excesses of a 15-year bull market could be "wrung out" in the space of a few months!

(7) Stocks Are Cheap

Traders look at a number of gauges of investor sentiment to determine what the market is going to do next. Since most investors (and investment advisors) are usually wrong at market extremes, these indicators are contrarian in nature—the more bullish the average investor is, the more bearish the trader becomes.

An awesome complacency showed itself in the progress of the bear market through 2000. As stocks fell, traders were disturbed by the repeated instances of concentrated selling without a true selling panic. The VIX and other key climactic indicators repeatedly gave bullish technical readings, but didn't scream "buy" the way they had in 1998.

As the market tumbled, investor optimism also fell—only to rebound periodically, as investors concluded that the next "big" rally was just around the corner. Apparently the damage to their equity portfolios, while significant, hardly warranted the "drastic" action of selling stock!

Millions of investors appeared unaware (or unwilling to admit?) that stocks were (or ever had been) overpriced. In 2000, most failed to recognize that a self-reinforcing, severely asset-debilitating bear market spiral had commenced, in which stock prices and P/E ratios were falling *together*.

Stocks didn't get "cheap," even after falling as much as 99 percent from their highs. The problem remained one of valuation. When judged by their P/E ratios, quite a few stocks had become *more* expensive at the end of 2000 than they had been at the beginning of the year—even though their prices had been generously marked down. Judging by the mania highs, stocks had become bargain-priced, but in relation to the historical mean, they offered less *value* than ever.

The problem wasn't just that earnings were falling along with stock prices—earnings were falling *faster* than stock prices. (These were the same earnings that, during the manic phase of the bull market, had sent investors into such ecstasies.)

All the way through the top, tech earnings remained terrific, and they didn't deteriorate significantly until the fourth quarter, when, one after another, the corporate behemoths "pre-warned" of earnings shortfalls—or, simply dropped crummy news on shareholders without warning.

The same creative accounting tricks which had contributed to stunning earnings in the midst of the bubble worked to pull those earnings down even more quickly in the bubble's aftermath. Profits from securities transactions quickly became losses; surging revenues quickly became shortfalls. As soon as insiders realized it was open season for writing off mistakes, the bad news suddenly began flooding in. Having been duly uttered by the Great Greenspan himself, the phrase "reduction in capital spending" was suddenly on the lips of corporate insiders—a perfect exculpatory dodge. After hedging or dumping their own stock, many corporate insiders discovered in the economic downturn an extraordinary opportunity to write off "special charges." (There's nothing like having an exogenous agent to blame for your errors.)

The very speed with which these companies deteriorated indicated the financial shabbiness of the underlying business . . . by spring 2001 they were writing off multi-billion dollar "goodwill on acquisitions" charges for the companies they had voraciously gobbled up during the mania phase in a misguided belief that market share was everything. All those vendor financing dodges also came back to haunt corporate financial statements as "sales" that were actually loans, which turned into *bad* loans.

As if directed by the wand of an offstage conductor, the incredibly sweet-smelling fundamentals, which had lasted so long, quickly soured: Long-distance bandwidth prices went into free fall, DRAM prices took a dive, B2B solutions were suddenly not nearly as compelling, and telecommunication giants began defaulting on their bonds.

Yet in April 2001, the market turned around. P/E ratios were deteriorating, but investors apparently didn't care—their bullishness was a disquieting reminder that *all* of the excesses hadn't been wrung out of the market, after all.

9
To The Rescue

> "Will the Commandant attend the execution?" "It is not certain," said the officer, wincing at the direct question, and his friendly expression darkened.
>
> —Franz Kafka, *Penal Colony*

The benevolent overseer of the asset-inflating economic regime of the 1990s was Alan Greenspan himself. In the Fed chairman, the market had a man who was willing to administer it a fresh goosing of liquidity whenever it needed it—in the jargon of the Street, he was "aggressively accommodating."

It seemed the Blessed Protector intervened in the marketplace almost monthly, dousing fires ignited by ruptured hedge funds and IMF basket cases. The list was long—a sorry liturgy of Statist dreams gone awry and moguls gone bust. All hearts beat a little quicker, knowing that between the soaring urges of Capital and the bottomless abyss of shrinking asset values stood *Greenspan*, like a great vigilant centurion.

Oh, well, every cult has its high priests. *Why not the Cult of Equities?*

In the autumn of 1998, Greenspan saved the world from itself yet again. After watching that heroic performance, market participants were sure that they had a genuine savior on their hands.

Had the Fed—in the earthly form of the Magnificent One, Greenspan—really discovered the secret to keeping the economy on a permanently even keel? Or had temporarily eye-popping productivity numbers, largely bubble-induced, lulled the chairman into leaving the nation's money taps permanently open?

For those with neither the time nor the inclination to study the market, its ups and downs can appear as unfathomable as nature itself. Only the high priest, Greenspan, is viewed as privy to these mysteries.

By 1999, some market participants understood that things were getting well out of hand, yet greed was still too much in the driver's seat for them to care much. People were on an unsustainable stock-buying binge, but so what? None of that mattered, because the Salvation Scenario remained in place. The Scenario, implicitly assumed by market participants at all times, featured the Fed arriving in time to save the day with *interest rate cuts*. Investors placed a premium on the Fed's willingness to limit market declines through its benign intervention.

To those unfamiliar with the corrupt processes at work, it might seem somewhat strange that those nominally charged with correcting market excesses instead created the very conditions for them. The "Greenspan Put," as it was called, contributed to the bubble to the exact degree that it sought to prevent its collapse; the Greenspan Put was, in fact, one of the bubble's *preconditions*.

In 1998, the Federal Reserve orchestrated the rescue of LTCM, a development to which we alluded earlier. That particular hedge fund-run-amok had, during its go-go years, profited vastly from the undertaking of risk on a grand scale—and so had those who had invested in it. But then LTCM nearly succumbed to the risk. In repairing the ensuing damage, the Fed showed the kind of attentiveness that only the billionaire class deserves.

On 1 October, 1998, Greenspan tried to justify the intervention by telling a congressional banking committee, "Financial market participants were already unsettled by recent global events. Had the failure of LTCM triggered the seizing up of markets, substantial damage could have been inflicted," and the "economies of many nations" could have been "potentially impaired."[1]

In 1984, Todd Conover, Comptroller of the Currency, had offered a similar rationale for an earlier intervention when he advised Congress that "had Continental [Bank] failed . . . we could very well have seen a national, if not an international, financial crisis the dimensions of which were difficult to imagine. None of us wanted to find out."[2]

Reading Conover's remarkable statement, one cannot help wondering which was the more frightening: An international financial crisis so severe that a Comptroller of the Currency cannot even imagine it—or a Comptroller of the Currency who is incapable of imagining a severe financial crisis.[3]

The economy is obviously far more fragile than most public officials are usually willing to admit. Greenspan was being less than fully candid when he described the LTCM rescue package as necessary to prevent the "seizing up of markets." In fact, a liquidity crisis had *already* occurred before LTCM was bailed out. Indeed, the reason LTCM needed to be rescued in the first place was that it had been unable to liquidate its positions.

How had "the economies of many nations" grown so "fragile" and so vulnerable that the blow-up of a hedge fund for millionaires risked "serious market dislocations"? What were the causes of the mysterious "recent global events" which had so "unsettled" unnamed market participants?

How could the implosion of a hedge fund which, according to the chairman, "limit[ed] its clientele to a small number of highly sophisticated, very wealthy individuals," jeopardize the whole enchilada?

Greenspan responded narrowly by referring to certain "cross-default clauses" which might infect other firms with the LTCM disease. But he did not expand his analysis, for he himself was far too complicit in the explosion of derivatives to offer a total critique of them.[4]

With a career bureaucrat's sure instinct for deflecting criticism, the chairman revealed that he was chiefly interested in defending his own flawed decision-making processes: "The Federal Reserve provided its good offices to LTCM's creditors, not to protect LTCM's investors, creditors, or managers from loss," (of course not!) "but to avoid the distortions to market processes caused by a fire sale liquidation and the consequent spreading of those distortions through contagion."

The spreading of distortions through contagion—that sounds like something out of a medical suspense novel. The chairman professed himself deeply chagrined at the thought that "market processes" might be "distorted" by "fire sale liquidation," thereby pretending that somehow all the "market processes" had started out pure. In fact, the business practices of such hedge funds routinely cause economic "distortions" far greater than any "fire sale."

Hmmm, we wouldn't want to distort any "market processes," now would we? For example, by squeezing the entire bond auction of a sovereign nation?

In his book *Inventing Money*, Nicholas Dunbar noted that at one August 1994 Italian government bond auction, LTCM participated in a "turkey shoot . . . driving up prices wasn't difficult . . . the banks were forced to go cap in hand to . . . traders at LTCM, paying high prices for the bonds. Insurance companies forced by law to invest in the bonds also fell victim to the squeeze."[5]

There was also the question of how many "distortions" Greenspan's LTCM fire-fighting efforts *incited*. In his October 1998 testimony, Greenspan (vaguely) addressed the issue, saying "To be sure, investors wiped out in a fire sale will clearly be less risk prone than if their mistakes were unwound in a more orderly fashion. But is the broader market well served if the resulting fear and other irrational judgments govern the degree of risk participants are subsequently willing to incur?"

The chairman might do well asking himself that again in 2001, since it is now clear that he helped kindle the worst bubble in 60 years by applying this flawed reasoning. All through 1999, investors remained in a kind of blissful daze, the cool wind of pure liquidity blowing through their hair. This blessed flock was possessed by the certain knowledge that the Fed stood in eternal preparedness to rescue *their* chestnuts from any speculative fire.

Greenspan erred on the *wrong* side: It wasn't "fear and other irrational judgments" which were to govern investor risk-tolerance for 18 months after these remarks were made; it was *greed* "and other irrational judgments."

Perhaps the most remarkable instance of blinder-clad thinking in Greenspan's testimony was the statement, "The prices received in a time of stress do not reflect longer-run potential . . ."

Apparently the chairman didn't stop to ask himself whether positions which were so speculative as to be subject to liquidation in panic market conditions might not, for that very reason, be worth far *less* than the market said they were worth at every other time.

Perhaps the "fire sale" or distressed price was the *proper* price—but that was almost unthinkable. By focusing strictly on the short-term costs of "fire sale liquidation," the chairman glossed over the positive effects that the departure of excessively-leveraged players from the market could have—such as dampening extreme speculation. In the case of LTCM, the market would have accomplished that task all by itself, despite being all "seized up," if only the meddlesome chairman had let it.

The message which the LTCM bailout sent to market participants was disastrously indiscreet: If you are big enough, the government will rescue you from your own excessive risk taking. (Little guys can hang.)

Afterwards, it was as if a new natural resource had been opened up for general exploitation, and everyone was determined to get their share before every well had been sucked dry. To some observers, it seemed a shame that the resource being debased was, in fact, the "full faith and credit" of the United States Government. Adding farce to the tragic mix was the debasement of faith in favor of doomed Internet startups and other short-range rockets.

Did the Magnificent One, Greenspan, really have to save mankind from the ravages of world depression *so regularly?* Why were leading economies so vulnerable to "seizing up," and what did this say about the "fragility" of world-capitalism? And if "serious market dislocations" were in regular danger of being "triggered," why had markets been rallying wildly for nearly the entire decade?

Was the chairman saving America by continually tinkering with its money supply—or were these moves expensive, but ultimately doomed, attempts to maintain an unsustainable economic boom?

Little has changed since the LTCM bailout, in spite of the giant bubble which ensued thereafter. Judging from the minutes of FOMC meetings, it has never occurred to these august bankers that, after the bubble and all the structural imbalances it caused, a serious economic slowdown might (gasp!) be a *necessary* thing—although certainly not a *desirable* one, in the view of most working Americans. They failed to recognize that future asset health depended on asset *liquidation*. The unwinding of overblown assets would be a good thing for the long-term health of an equilibrium-seeking market—if not for the citizens who too unscrupulously submit themselves to it.

In any case, a "good" outcome is hardly possible these days. It's more a question of whether the excesses of a bubble economy dissipate rapidly or linger on—kind of like the choice between tearing off a bandage that is stuck to your skin quickly or slowly. Fast hurts, but it is over with quickly; the slow way drags the pain out almost indefinitely—just ask the Japanese.

To pull America out of its post-millennial doldrums, Greenspan wanted American consumers to intensify their already-voracious consumerism, but perhaps what *they* needed to do was *stop* spending and begin saving a little more (gasp again!). A higher savings rate was a prerequisite for economic health, but it was looking as if Americans wouldn't stop their spending until they were dealt a hand of financial cards so bad that they had to . . . fold.

Savings rates tend to revert to the mean; there is no substitute for "austerity" when one has already blown one's wad.[6] Lest this remark be taken as advocacy for government intervention, we hasten to add that the intervention of bureaucrats is not required; the market will do the job itself, victims be damned—as usual.

10
Hyperactivity in High Places

Let the value of all things be posited newly by you.

—Friedrich Nietzsche, *Thus Spoke Zarathustra*

Through most of 2000, the economy acted like a 99-year-old man on pep-pills: It was still racing, but it looked like it was about to croak. The Fed was noticeably concerned about its prize patient, but in its eagerness to revive it, the Fed was overdosing on the pain medicine. No sooner had the Fed completed a rushed tightening cycle than it embarked on an unprecedented easing cycle. Presumably this was done, not in the service of the American citizenry, but of those unspecified market players who were again in 2000 quite "unsettled" by the prospect of "serious market dislocations"—that is to say, by the prospect of lower returns on their investments.

When did Greenspan's mandate change from keeping the economy in line to keeping the Bears at bay? The Federal Reserve's job is to maintain the stability of the financial system—not to maintain a boom at all costs. Yet the 2001 rate cuts (some of which were dropped on the market as "surprises" with the equities markets only days from catastrophic collapse) were clearly designed to inflict maximum pain on the shorts—surgical strikes on bear positions.[1]

Again and again, the chairman has insisted that monetary policy isn't dictated by the gyrations of the market. Yet as he has frequently revealed, he looks at *price*, which reflects investor expectations, for clues as to the future direction of the economy. For example, he enjoys expounding upon the backwardation or contango relationships of oil futures contracts.

Perhaps it is to surmount this intolerable contradiction—between a Greenspan who pretends to stand above the market and one who is slavishly dependent upon it—that he has become, over the years, a frequent dabbler in the markets: A sort of swing-trader in the bond futures pits of Chicago.

The Federal funds futures contract anticipates the Federal funds rate, which is determined by the FOMC. With few exceptions, the bond markets anticipate Greenspan's moves so thoroughly that it would be more accurate to say that they *cause* them. Traders like *any* excuse for volatility, and Greenspan is more often the excuse than the cause for it.

The generalized assertion of the chairman's omnipotence, the palpable fear allegedly felt by all market participants when they hear his elephantine steps echoing down Pennsylvania Avenue, the great respect which all traders are said to feel when listening to his ponderous speeches—these fictions are maintained for the purpose of buttressing "investor confidence." In fact, traders largely *fade* the chairman. (They do this, not by betting against him, but by "buying the rumor, selling the news.")

The sprightly septuagenarian is far too dependent on the markets to front-jump them. He seldom even tries anymore, because such efforts would have only shock-value. And there is always the risk that fruitless rate cuts could cast a pall over the chairman's carefully-cultivated aura—that would be bad.

In early 2001, the Fed eased money five times, but credit markets sabotaged these profligate gestures by blowing out the spreads on corporate bonds and steepening the curve on government fixed-income instruments. Money had been made cheaper, but banks were simultaneously tightening their lending standards, especially to commercial borrowers—just the sort of thing that gives central bankers gray hair.

Was it pure recklessness, pure fear, or pure ignorance of the risk of reflating the bubble, that drove the Fed to slash interest rates 250 basis points in the first five months of 2001? The answer—and here we are being charitable—is none of the above. When the illusory appearance of omnipotence is stripped away, we see that Greenspan and his banking cronies are men who no longer hope to *control* anything; they merely wish to keep the whole thing *going*.

Why the desperate interest-rate cutting? Bankers feed the maw of the great creature because they have no other choice; as soon as they stop stuffing it, it begins to die.

11
Exit Stage Right

Après moi, le déluge.

—Louis XV

Finance, *n.* The art or science of managing revenues and resources for the best advantage of the manager.

—Ambrose Bierce

Wall Street has never had any respect for the individual investor—it *fades* individual investors, and has done so for years.

The strategy is a flexible one: *Get 'em coming and going.*

The securities business is so darned profitable during bull market runs, all other money-making scenarios pale in comparison. According to the Greater Fool theory, higher equity prices will be met with ever-bigger fools—*ad infinitum.* Trading on this cynical strategy presupposes the impossible, yet during the bubble of the 1990s, it worked splendidly!

But by the time the 1990s ended, middle-class investors were about as fully committed as they were ever going to be. Colossal success had presented the Boys, who are largely dependent on a rising sea of middle-class money to keep the market (not to mention themselves) afloat, with a serious dilemma: Where would the money come from to fuel the next leg of the rally?

The amazing run-up had lifted bad stocks and good alike on a tide of dollars, but the Boys who were still long equities were exposed to a very large degree of systemic risk. Venture capitalists, underwriters, and corporate insiders, among others, understood this. They were still sitting atop a mountain of paper assets, but the rally was showing distinct signs of cracking, and they were worried about the downside risk.

The Boys tend to be considerably more cynical and considerably less "exuberant" about stocks than average investors, and they'd had one hell of a ride. The "pump" phase had been milked to death, so it was time to "dump." What better place to slough off risk than a stock exchange filled with dip-buying investors?

The doomed advances of 2000, each of which made lower highs, were classic bear market rallies, and they were for selling into. The rallies enabled the Boys to scale into their shorts at excellent prices.

Commitment of Traders reports issued by the Commodity Futures Trading Commission (CFTC) track changes in open interest among various investor categories, and these reports clearly show the pace at which the "commercials," or hedging traders, extricated themselves from the dangers presented by the bubble. The commercials, who have a dependably excellent track record (in contrast to the "small speculative" class of traders), went net-short S&P 500 index futures within spitting distance of the top and continued selling throughout the summer and fall—selling, even as the pundits from the equity research departments were blandly predicting a bounce.

Corporate insiders also sold stock at a record pace through 2000. The cleverest employed zero-cost collars as a way of establishing a minimum value, or "floor," for their holdings, thereby effectively locking in the mania price. They would have to surrender their stock to a counterparty if their company's stock accrued further price gains, but these insiders weren't terribly concerned about that, and by making this small concession, they raked in as much in premiums as they shelled out (hence the name "zero-cost" collar). These options cost them almost nothing! *What could be sweeter?*

The intricate ploy served its purpose: It created a barrier, or "fence," between those who now had the money of the middle class and the middle class itself, which was starting to want it back. Corporate insiders were determined not to return a penny of their fabulous gains back to those who had invested in their companies, often on the alleged "strength of the management team"!

Gee, the insiders must have had a premonition that the stock prices of their companies were about to crash.

12
Great White Sharks

> Stocks are manipulated to the highest point possible and then sold to the public on the way down.
>
> —Jesse Livermore

What does it all add up to, the amazing 1990s bull market? To a shift of *trillions* of U.S. dollars from weak hands to strong ones. A mountain of money passed from the pockets of credulous buyers to those of skeptical sellers.

The term "distribution" has been defined as "the entire process by which in the course of a public offering [a] block of securities is dispersed and ultimately comes to rest in the hands of the investing public."[1]

Such a transfer must be widely deemed as "just," so that those who end up getting stuck with shrunken paper don't have a leg to stand on when they start to complain. The Boys had reduced their potential liabilities on this count by having investors sign papers saying they understood just how much risk they were taking on.

We are tracing legal versions of that otherwise highly illegal activity, the pump and dump—hyping a stock in order to profit from a long position in it. The technique was perfected at "bucket shops" and Internet chat sites by an assortment of minor scam artists. Their relatively tiny bankrolls meant that they could only fiddle with stocks that had tiny floats—they were bottom-feeders, not Great Whites.

Atop the predatory chain sat the investment houses. Thanks to the magnanimousness of the government and the awesome power of leverage, their capital resources were practically unlimited. These banks were able to vastly improve upon traditional bucket shop methods by lending them a patina of respectability. And instead of a few thousand suckers, they had half the American population on the hook!

It was a delicious opportunity, and the Giants of Finance were determined to make the most of it.

The Boys' *modus operandi* wasn't all that much different from the one they had employed all of the other times, during the Age of the Hostile Takeover and the Savings and Loan (S&L) Scandal and the Real Estate Booms: Risk somebody else's capital while reaping windfall profits for yourself, then depart in the nick of time—a delicate task, but the Boys have always been up to it.

Smart money skunked foolish money. It wasn't the first time.

When the stock market is dropping, it's funny how quickly the interests of big money and small investors diverge. In 1999, the Boys stayed long as the public bid stocks up to unsustainable levels, then as the herd began shuffling politely (too politely) towards the exit, the Boys sold the market short to lock in their gains.

They turned everything into grist for their hype-mill—the breezy news tone, the unflappable optimism, the absurd earnings forecasts, all of which were based on bubble-era performance continuing forever.

The entire edifice seemed rock-like and unshakeable—until the first cracks appeared. These quickly widened and soon the whole dubious enterprise was at risk.

Oh yeah, the Boys set America up—but then, that *is* their profession.

13
That Sinking Feeling

The identity of idea and reality is denied by reality . . .

—Theodor Adorno, *Negative Dialectics*

Japan's economy is in rotten shape, and it has been like that for a decade. As Japan's officials have openly acknowledged, all efforts at jump-starting the economy have been unsuccessful to date.

The Japanese experience demonstrates the way in which bubbles can plant a series of economic time-bombs, some of which "accidentally" explode only much later. In Japan, gross government incompetence was piled on top of investor greed. Instead of allowing their bubble to die a thorough (if thoroughly graceless) death, functionaries put it on permanent life support. In the process, they emptied the national treasury while burdening future generations with unprecedented levels of national debt, thereby systematically turning the country into one gigantic, lousy credit risk.

As befitted a nation seemingly prone to periodic fits of idealist distemper, the Japanese bubble of the 1980s easily outdid America's more sedate 1990s version. The Japanese bubble was a *glorious* bubble.

The problem was the awful hangover which followed—it just wouldn't go away! In 2001, the Nikkei Index was trading at levels last seen in the 1980s. Those who remained invested in Japanese stocks were granted ample opportunity to mourn their steadfastness.

A lot of investors assume that a cut in interest rates automatically stimulates an economy; the Japanese case suggests otherwise. As Japanese central bankers have been (slowly) learning, cheaper money is no panacea for the aftermath of a bubble. They dropped interest rates to *zero* without stimulating economic growth.

This might happen, warned John Maynard Keynes. With the Great Depression in mind, he noted that under certain conditions, lowering short-term interest rates might not help an economy. He dubbed this predicament a "liquidity trap." The central bank spews out money like a great beached whale, but risk-adverse players detour that money into bonds or cash; money earmarked to stimulate the economy is effectively sucked into a black hole.

In the past, when the American economy has first emerged from the trough of a recession, credit had an almost magical effect on it. Businesses are famished for credit, and a dollar of new loans "yields" two dollars in growth. At the end of a bull market, however, this ratio is reversed, and it takes two or three dollars of new loans to generate a single dollar of new growth. The problem isn't liquidity—the problem is finding borrowers credit-worthy enough to loan money to.

As the U.S. economy slumped into early 2001, some economists worried that a liquidity trap might be developing. Greenspan, for his part, was determined to head off a deflationary spiral, even if it meant risking inflation. He opened the money taps at a time when the economy was already suffering from a glut of the green stuff.

Wall Street would have expected nothing less.

14
The Sound of **it Hitting the Fan

The bulls enter through the *puerta de toriles* (door of the bullpens). Over it, before each fight, is placed a sign that shows the bull's name, his brand number, and his weight in kilograms.

—Homer Casteel, Jr., *Running of the Bulls*

It'll be interesting to see who's going to be blamed for the mess—because somebody is going to get blamed sooner or later—bet on it.

Merely to be theoretically consistent, those working inside politics *must* identify an exogenous agent on whom to pin the blame for all problems, because, by definition, for these agents to submit the system they operate in to the level of criticism required to recognize, let alone repair, its structural (internal) deficiencies would entail subjecting their *own* positions to scrutiny, and this they are understandably loathe to do.

Those in search of scapegoats will find few volunteers among the beneficiaries of the bull market.

We don't expect VCs to admit that much of what they were churning out on the IPO treadmill was utter garbage. Can they really be blamed for giving investors what they wanted—and giving it to them in spades?

Stockbrokers weren't about to step forward at the height of the mania and point out to clients that stocks were absurdly overpriced—clients sitting in cash generate no commissions. Analysts weren't willing to admit that they were colossally mistaken when they raised price targets going into Y2K, while the investment houses that promoted their bullish fantasies continued collecting fat fees.

Yes, they manipulated—or shall we say, "managed"—the situation in order to yield the largest possible profit to themselves. But can they really be faulted for scooping up the gold while it lay in the streets?

Or should we place responsibility at the doorstep of short-term speculators? They were perhaps the least responsible; in their single-minded pursuit of profit, they weren't burdened with the long-term investor's dogmatic perspective. They arbitraged the mispricing they found in the market, but they didn't create it.

Or is Alan Greenspan to blame? Those who think the excesses of a decade can be corrected by the prudence of one man may well end up scapegoating him—but what is he guilty of?

On 5 December 1996, when the Fed chairman famously cautioned against "irrational exuberance," he was placing in the historical record an official protest—partly a warning, mostly a disclaimer—against excessive speculation, and he was doing it ahead of a process he was largely powerless to bring to a happy conclusion.

His failing lay in permitting himself the conceit of imagining that he could smooth out the business cycle's rough edges by tinkering with the aggregates. But hubris is a character deficiency, not a crime.

Nor do we expect middle-class investors to admit that they were wrong in throwing wads of money after over-bred racehorses without taking the time to thoroughly understand what they were investing in. Besides, who can fault them for "buying in"? The price gains *were* enticing, while they lasted.

With average life expectancy increasing, medical costs spiraling out of control, and pensions largely a thing of the past, Americans decided that they had to keep adding to their 401Ks if they were to retire comfortably.

Unfortunately, the comfortable golden years Americans routinely expected as their just reward were "guaranteed" by many of the same stocks which swooned so spectacularly in the spring of 2000.[1]

Of course, by bidding prices up past all sensible levels, middle-class investors actively contributed to their own financial decline. In the 1990s they were riding the crest of a bubble, and for a while they seemed to like it just fine. Seeking relational advantage within an existing system, they never stopped to question the basic arrangements. That's the marvelous thing about greed in America: No matter how egregious it is, it remains entirely forgivable, according to the social ethic which prevails—even laudable.

Besides, a hundred million investors can't *all* be criminally greedy, now can they?

15
The Same Boat?

> The poor person, even if he possesses only one Thaler, can participate in the holding of public stock which is divided into very small portions, and can thus speak of *our* palaces, *our* factories, *our* treasures.
>
> —Charles Fourier

It would be possible to trace the relationship between capital and labor through its many troubled phases over the last four or five hundred years; here we can do no more than skim the surface of that relationship.

Already in the nineteenth century, the virtues of public stock ownership had been grasped by a few clever people in the court circles of latter-day European monarchs (where capitalist interests were already well represented) as a possible way to quell the social "malaise" of the time.

Towards the end of the nineteenth century, the Red Specter hovered over Europe's palaces and boardrooms like a menace, and the risk of social revolution seemed very real. Workers didn't feel like they were part of the system—and no wonder, because most of them weren't. Badly shaken by the fury unleashed in the 1848 Revolutions, enterprise owners realized that they needed to offer labor something appealing, if revolutionary sentiment was to be contained. Astute observers understood that broad public ownership of stock would have the effect of legitimizing the corporations in which money was invested, and by extension, the entire economic system.

Until the 1920s, the financial markets remained largely the playground of the rich. In the excitement of that decade, many Americans speculated in the markets for the first time. With the 1929 crash, however, the common Joe forsook equities, and he would not return to them for decades.

During the 1930s, union officials took a typically antagonistic stance towards employers, viewing most compromises with them as potentially ruinous. Labor was anti-capital because it was sure that capital was anti-labor, and capital was anti-labor because it wanted the best returns it could get on its dollar. It was believed that paying workers "too much" was bad for business; if workers weren't paid enough, however, they were likely to end up on the picket line.

The great seduction of America began in earnest in the 1950s, with the advent of a whole shiny new world of consumer appliances. In the kitchen, a housewife's life was "made easier by modern science"—or at least, that was what the television was telling her, over and over and over again. But beyond the gleaming linoleum confines of the family kitchen, new technologies were a decidedly mixed blessing.

The "deal" that existed implicitly between American workers and employers went something like this: Labor would be compensated for its political and social quiescence with a reasonably lucrative wage and benefits package. The possibility of home ownership was an intrinsic part of the deal, as were, increasingly, employee stock options. The deal was also implicitly revocable. If workers failed to gain what they judged to be sufficient personal advantage in compensation for acting as if their employer's fortunes were their own, they could strike—or, for that matter, take the difference out of the employer's pocket through absenteeism, pilferage, or the stealing back of their own time on the job.

By the 1970s, mechanization was permitting employers to eliminate workers. The threat to automate the factory was a potent one, and in labor negotiations it gave employers the edge they were looking for.

Soon working Americans were suffering from more than their wholesale replacement by machines. The nation's fascination with the internal combustion engine, its unquenchable thirst for crude oil, and the latent drag of paying for its failed military ventures, combined to set off a powerful inflationary spiral. Real-estate speculators and "gold bugs" happily rode the inflation all the way to the moon; others weren't as prescient. In fact, the savings of an entire generation of retirees were decimated during the 1970s and early 1980s.

When Americans elected Hollywood movie star Ronald Reagan to the highest office in the land, they elected a champion of the free markets. But they were also voting for big money, even if they did not always realize it. For his part, the Gipper was determined to give the ailing U.S. economy the shot of free enterprise he believed it needed. That wouldn't be an easy task. After years of stock and bond market underperformance, it was going to take some eye-popping profits to get people investing *en masse* again.

The gravel-voiced impresario represented narrow business interests bent on dismantling the unions—the PATCO affair was only the most notorious example. But the offensive against the unions was also an attack on the middle class itself. Although it seems almost strange to relate, at the time many factory workers were still part of the middle class! That wasn't quite efficient enough for the Reagan economists, who knew that the easiest way to boost corporate profits was to trim the lifestyles of a few tens of millions of wage workers.[1]

Corporations leveraged the resultant "downsizing" to the considerable profit of stockholders. From then on, enterprises waxed and swelled like budding fruit. Meanwhile, middle-class factory workers were reclassified as an endangered species, although they quickly adapted themselves to the new regime, finding work in the service economy—flipping hamburgers or selling real estate.

In the 1980s and 1990s, voters treated themselves three times to Presidents—Reagan, Bush Sr., and Bill Clinton—all of whom equated the interests of the American people with those of the multinational corporations. In the prevailing ethic, these interests were considered complementary, and all who doubted this were tarred "anti-business" (the bull-booster's favorite invective).

During their reign, the Hollywood-hugging Democrats certainly betrayed the working classes to an extent that Republican leaders could only dream of matching. The Democratic Party was the traditional party of labor. It was trusted by labor—a fatal gullibility which gave those opportunistic elements which coalesced around Bill Clinton in 1992 the opportunity to betray working people while simultaneously pretending to uphold their interests. Coming from the Republicans, the betrayal would have been obvious.

In the sheer glibness of his socio-pathology, George W. Bush cannot match Clinton. There was only one president facile enough to preside over the ultimate bubble: William Jefferson Clinton.

In one of those slow seductions which at first are highly gratifying to those who surrender to them, the middle class wholeheartedly threw its lot in with big money—and by extension, accepted the ideology that accompanied it: Investing in yourself was investing in the market; investing in the market was investing in yourself. To oppose the corporation was to oppose the market—and that was considered crazy.

For the longest time, this complementarity of interests seemed to hold, but the stock market spasms of 2000-2001 risked the sort of disillusionment that people suffer from holding suddenly worthless investments.

The Six-Trillion-Dollar question was: *Would a really foul bear market cause the middle class to bow out of the grand alliance?*

While the reality of financial decline is difficult for almost anybody to accept, harder still is the *social* decline that usually accompanies it, as this threatens an individual's self-esteem. (Moving from, say, a six-bedroom house to an apartment block tends to hurt a person's confidence level.)

It seems hardly necessary to point out that, throughout history, a downwardly mobile middle class has been the human nursery of fascism.

16
Who, Me?

> The fall proves to everyone except him that he never participated in the numinous and that, like everyone else, he is subject to the laws of nature; the truth of this man is gravity, he is in bondage to it every bit as much as inert matter is.
>
> —Jean-Paul Sartre, *The Family Idiot*

Long before it occupied the White House, the incoming administration of G.W. Bush repeatedly denied that any of the nation's economic ills were *its* problems.

Had Republicans nothing to do with the recent stock-buying binges, the bidding-up of real estate to absurd levels, the depletion of the world's non-renewable energy resources, the colossal misallocation of capital, the credit bubble, or any of the other things which were so obviously ailing the economy?

No, nothing.

Bush is smug enough to disown all such problems, but that is to be expected. Like other leaders, and merely to represent his relatively narrow constituency, he must relegate the origin of all economic problems beyond the pale of his conceptual universe, that is to say, to the enemy camp; the crudely dualistic world-view to which he subscribes allows him no other choice.

As a Republican, Bush must insist that Republican policies uniformly result in a better world. All economic troubles *must* be placed at the Democrats' doorstep; admitting to any other possibility would be tantamount to political apostasy.

The over-availability of capital arising from profligate bank-lending practices, the overvaluation of the dollar, the explosion of credit derivatives, the Third World's financial inability to consume the products it makes, manufacturing overcapacity, overspending on information technology, the effect that dwindling strategic commodity prices have on supply during disinflationary economic phases—all these factors are systemic in nature. Yet to listen to Bush, it is as if these various mispricings, structural imbalances, weaknesses, stresses, shortages, and so on, have fallen from the sky.

Simply to maintain appearances, "optimists" such as President George W. Bush must deny that any systemic problems exist, for to admit their existence would require acknowledging that these are problems we have *all* created *together*—and in America, that would surely include Republicans as well as Democrats.

The Bush administration's effort to distance itself from the excesses of the 1990s is troubling, because until all parties acknowledge the underlying problem—the depredations implicit in the philosophy of growth-at-any-cost—there can be little hope of remedying it.

17
Gas and a Burger, Please

> In the face of the huge images spread across the walls of houses, where toothpaste and cosmetics lie handy for giants, sentimentality is restored to health and liberated in American style, just as people whom nothing moves or touches any longer are taught to cry again by films.
>
> —Walter Benjamin, *One-Way Street*

In March 2001, Bush promised to help solve a developing national energy crisis by encouraging more energy production. The fledgling president referred to energy shortages only euphemistically when he said, "Many Americans are struggling from the high price of energy."[1] But was it not rather the case that the world's resources were "struggling" with the American people, who are the most energy-profligate in the world?

The 5,000 sq. ft. houses, the 5,000 lb. SUVs, the frantic paving-over and subdividing of the land to construct miniature home-fortresses which are only dark caverns without a constant infusion of power—these had nothing to do with the escalating energy costs?

Nothing, if the utterances of George W. were any indication.

According to the philosophy of blind optimism, Americans should on no account be encouraged to do any soul-searching about their lifestyles. Yet a *symptom* is precisely that which is neither recognized nor affirmed. Repressing it does not prevent its eruption—on the contrary.[2]

While a few computer whizz-kids with nifty techno-toys were being turned into billionaires by the red-hot IPO market, little money had been spent on oil exploration or refining, on the construction of electric power plants, or on natural gas production facilities.

In California, that paradise-cum-shopping-mall, the incompetence of state energy regulators and legislators joined with corporate shortsightedness and greed to spawn a serious electricity crisis. To avoid widespread blackouts, state officials were forced to purchase electricity in the "spot" market, where they were unmercifully squeezed by traders. Before there could be any hope of financial solvency for California's utilities, residents would have to pay a lot more for electricity.

It was starting to occur to (a few) people that without a constant dose of energy, all their techno-trinkets would be completely useless. For years, computer marketers had been cannibalizing the vocabulary of the automobile industry ("turbo," "horsepower," etc.), but perhaps only a blacked-out California could fully expose the arrogance of jargon-distilling tech-boosters, or the dystopian character of their epiphanies.

It is upon such unconscious mechanisms, which are often mistaken for "coincidences," that we now focus.

The Bush Presidency itself was another of those unconscious forces. Bush did not win the election, exactly —in terms that Bill Clinton might appreciate, Bush "won" the election, well, sort of. It was all rather confusing, especially if you were watching the television networks on election night—their ridiculous bungling of the victory call(s) was another of those factors which seem to spring up, unbidden, in times of social and economic flux.

The curtain had been drawn back on the confidence-factory, and it was not a pretty sight.

Meanwhile, in the grim abattoirs and gleaming supermarkets of Europe, the threats to human carnivores were growing—mad cow, hoof-and-mouth, and *E. coli*. These maladies are significant even beyond the suffering they cause, because they arose in the context of the most merciless rationalization and subjugation of life in favor of economic production.

There is something sick about feeding cows "nutritional supplements" made from the rendered and dried carcasses of other cows and sheep—after all, cows are naturally vegetarian. Scientists believe this dubious technique may have been responsible for introducing mad cow disease into the livestock populations of Europe. It jumped to the human population sometime thereafter.

Meat manufacturers pump cows full of hormones and antibiotics, stick stunts into their brains on death-producing assembly lines (causing spillage of contaminated brain matter), then they slaughter the animals—but they don't inspect most of the carcasses (saving money), although doing so would keep thousands of their meat-eating customers from contracting illness. Finally, the meat industrialists don't waste a bit, recycling parts of the carcasses back for the next generation of livestock—even though the entire herd might have to be culled due to the fatal diseases it potentially harbors. Yes, *efficiency indeed!*

The moniker "mad cow disease" begs the question of whether it was the mad cows which infected the humans, or the humans who infected the cows with a strange form of human madness—just the kind of tragicomic drama that the growth-at-any-cost myth tends to foster. In mad cow and the slightly less objectionable hoof-and-mouth and *E. coli*, Westerners had their own pathologies delivered back to them—nicely shrink-wrapped in plastic and, of course, with the $ sign attached.

Is the transmogrification of human creativity into never-ending assembly lines which churn out record-setting amounts of increasingly toxic produce really the apogee of human civilization?

18
Turbo-Closet

> The capitalist appears as a fanatic agent of accumulation who seeks neither use-value nor *jouissance* . . .
>
> —Jean-Joseph Goux, *Symbolic Economies*

The acquisitive asset spree of the 1990s was accompanied by a voracious expansionism in all areas—something Edward Luttwak has dubbed "Turbo-Capitalism." The three-bedroom split-level homes of the *nouveaux riches*, which sprang up like unsightly fungi all across the valley known as Silicon, were only the most visible signs of the credit, real estate, and equity bubbles then well underway.

In its final stages, the mania was entirely dependent on investors who were driven—driven to the point where they couldn't sustain their mania-inducing investing style any longer. The sheer *urgency* of the need to buy assets (cost be damned) resulted in extraordinary buying panics, which marked a crisis in American consumerism—a "virtual" hysteria. Nothing demonstrated this better than the fabled

"IPO-day," on which cynical underwriters dropped shares of newly-printed stock into the laps of investors like Roman Emperors doling out gilded fig leaves to a demented mob.

By aggressively cutting interest rates at the beginning of 2001, by making what had already been laughably easy money even easier to get, the Federal Reserve continued to encourage that most peculiar of American proclivities: Spending Beyond One's Means.

For years, the credit card industry had been mailing unsolicited "checks" to cardholders with the suggestion that they use them to "consolidate [their] debt" or even "take a vacation." In 2001, the Fed was openly doing the same thing through its fiscal and monetary policies. Since Americans could scarcely take on much more debt, this amounted to an unprincipled provocation to buy—*pandering*.

The central bank's targeting of American citizens as its agent of redemption from its bubble-based economic imbroglios seems an almost cruel propensity. The taxpayer has *always* been tapped to bail out wayward enterprises which authorities have judged "too big to fail." But then, the excesses of individuals, no matter how egregious, are puny in comparison to those of the corporations.

Even as the number of personal bankruptcies surged 20 percent, Greenspan made money 25 percent cheaper to borrow—that's exactly the kind of prudence we expect from a banker, isn't it?

19
Shaky

> The constant equation between subject and commodity . . . drives up the narcissistic ante . . .
>
> —Robert Goldman and Stephen Papson, *Sign Wars*

The hyper-growth which (too many assumed) had became a permanent fixture on the economic horizon was itself predicated upon a continuous ethic of "shop-'till-you-drop" consumerism. But for that very reason, the economy was vulnerable if people ever *stopped* shopping. Since consumers accounted for two-thirds of the U.S. economy, if it was to keep growing they had to borrow more, invest more, and spend more—the whole shaky structure would implode if they stopped for even a week.

The imperative? *Americans had to exhaust themselves, earning and spending*. (The problem is, they already had.)

Going deeper into debt with each passing year—that had become nearly as American as buying war bonds had been in the 1940s. As 2001 advanced, revolving credit surged to new levels (of irresponsibility), leading some bears to wonder if Americans were hitting their unsecured credit lines for one last fling before declaring bankruptcy.

Meanwhile, the U.S. Congress was busy shutting off the escape hatch.

Congressmen described the pre-existing bankruptcy code as a "loophole," but keen observers of the morass in Washington have long been aware that such loopholes aren't flaws in the original legislation, nor are they one day suddenly "discovered" by zealous lawmakers and then quickly purged from the Federal canon. Most loopholes are put there for a reason—they are in somebody's interest. They get eliminated through similar determinations.

The timing of the "loophole-tightening" legislation was hardly accidental, since for the first time quite large numbers of middle class investors (rather than rich scamsters) might actually be in need of those protections.

From an authoritarian perspective, Congress's sudden concern over widespread "abuse" of the bankruptcy laws must be rated a grim but necessary measure. Without gutting the law, the existing financial system might not survive the strain of the very large number of personal bankruptcies which a deep economic recession would bring.

Apparently congressmen can read tea leaves perfectly well when they feel like it.

20
Trickle Where?

> The absence of the sender, the addressor, from the marks that he abandons, which are cut off from him and continue to produce effects beyond his presence . . .
>
> —Jacques Derrida, *Signature Event Context*

How much did middle-class Americans benefit from the rise? Personal income rose—but so did personal spending, which easily kept up. What mattered wasn't how much Americans had already blown—and it was a bundle; what mattered was how much they still had in their wallets—and there wasn't much left.

By 1998, the U.S. economic system had proved far less effective at *creating* national wealth than it had at concentrating it. Between 1989 and 1997—during the accumulation phase—86 percent of the gigantic stock market gains went into the coffers of the richest 10 percent of households.[1] At the extremes, the numbers were even more shocking: By 1998, Bill Gates was richer than the poorest 45 percent of American households *combined!*[2]

Americans were narrowly rewarded for investing in the stock market during the go-go years—we say "narrowly," because most of those who reaped significant short-term rewards simultaneously took on more debt. The full scale of their indebtedness is not apparent until the increase in *public* debt is also factored in. Then we see the full effect of the wealth transfer. Somehow, at the end of 20 years of "trickling down," wealthy bond owners were holding IOUs that the government had signed on behalf of the American people, who now had to make good on them all.

Instead of the money trickling down, as the Reagan economists had promised it would, most of it seemed to have trickled *up*. The net worth of all but the richest Americans *fell* from 1983 to 1997.[3] Americans had taken on additional debt—several trillion dollars more, if you counted the U.S. budget deficits run-up since the Reagan-era reflation began.

Over in the Asset-Backed Securities (ABS) market, they were peddling the signed-and-sealed obligations of the middle class to the highest bidder.

Good old-fashioned credit card receivables—the same ones which people default on when they declare bankruptcy—are one of the bulwarks of the ABS market.

Credit card users can spend up to the limit of their unsecured credit lines—a happy development, at least, for those reaping the returns, who remain tranquil as long as Americans are willing and able to service 18 or 21 percent annualized interest rate burdens.

During the home refinancing binges of 1998 and 1999 alone, Americans cashed out $55 billion.[4] Average citizens had been lured by the promise of perpetual prosperity into pledging up their home equity to finance companies and banks and credit card issuers in exchange for some quick cash.

Over the years, banking and financial institutions had become mere conduits of risk, selling or "sponsoring" the risk they undertook through the securitization pipeline.

When ABS were brought into the same valuational universe as other credit instruments (through the rating system), the investment quality of *all* credit instruments—even Treasuries—was potentially eroded.[5] When middle-class Americans began declaring bankruptcy in higher numbers —as happened in 2000-2001—buyers of ABS started pricing in higher risk premiums.

Institutions naturally seek to enhance the credit of an asset-backed security they're bringing to market in various ways, often of the "contain the contagion" variety.[6] They spend a great deal of time trying to anticipate how ABS collateral will behave under stress, but in the last resort, the "collateral" in question, and which they sell so profitably, is the human being!

The risk that debtors will default is priced into the ABS market, and expectations as to the future performance of debtor-class workhorses are reflected in spreads that are electronically updated every few seconds on trading screens around the world. The willingness and ability of the debtor class to keep making its monthly payments is itself handicapped by the market.

Yes, people have been "repackaged" into interest-bearing investments. If financial institutions were to apply strict truth-in-advertising standards to their ABS dealings, they would have to end their pretense by slapping a label on the foreheads of Jane and Joe: RENT ME FOR 20 YEARS AT $20/hr.

We do not expect to see that anytime soon, since here as always, the wealthy are intent on covering up all traces that lead to the source of their wealth, that is to say, it must appear as if capital, and not the human being, produces the wealth.

21
Hardcore Junkie

> Getting the needles fixed in the glass was a technical problem, but after many experiments we overcame the difficulty. No trouble was too great for us to take, you see.
>
> —Franz Kafka, *Penal Colony*

During its go-go years the economy became addicted to nonstop growth; severe withdrawal pains were to be expected when the happy gas was finally cut off. Things had reached such a point that, if Americans merely started saving 2 or 3 percent of their income (instead of spending what they had and borrowing even more), they would send the economy into a tailspin. Frugality was now disastrous for the nation!

Yet overcapacity—a glut of goods so immense that even the closets and basements of Americans were not capacious enough to hold it all—threatened to overwhelm even the most ardent of shoppers.

The overcapacity showed up in government releases under Greenspan's preferred aliases for it: "Inventory correction" and "pronounced lack of pricing power."

Behind all the rigmarole about "consumer confidence" lies this unpleasant truth: It isn't Jane and Joe's earning or spending power which ultimately supports the grand financial house of cards in all of its parasitical splendor—it is the *productive capacity* of their labor. No wonder, then, that so many investments have been "structured" to sag expressly upon Jane and Joe's shoulders.

Material wealth is neither an alchemic by-product of financial speculation nor the result of technological progress *per se*; it is the result of concerted human labor and applied ingenuity. But we must remember that, as in all confidence games, the trick here for the rip-off specialist is to do nothing which might rattle the confidence level of the "mark." The illusion that money is the source of all wealth must be maintained at all costs.

When Greenspan says, "Risk taking is a necessary condition of wealth creation,"[1] one has to wonder—is the chairman defending Americans, or the interests of Wall Street? The financial sector has become so entrenched in the society that one has to go back to Eisenhower's famous "military-industrial complex" of the 1950s and 1960s to find a proper analogy for it.

Financial institutions have been packaging and selling more than just stock these past decades; they have been packaging and selling the middle class itself. The All Sales Are Final approach to risk management works brilliantly at the cusp of a bull market.[2]

When "Let your profits ride" stops resonating inside investor craniums, there's only one way to maintain corporate profits. Unable to entice high-risk capital any longer, financial institutions must set to colonizing their respective cash-flow strata, stratum by stratum.

There is nothing finer than a cash-flow stratum that performs robustly—as long it keeps performing, of course. With the sideshow in equities suddenly made less compelling, it was time to return to the old standby—installment-plan capitalism. If the 1980s were the Age of the Corporate Takeover and the 1990s were the Age of the Dotcom, the first decade of the new millennium might well be dubbed the Age of the Rent-For-Life Age—the point at which the whole global economy becomes *one gigantic parking-meter.*

Rent for life? Perhaps Rent*ed*-For-Life is a better expression, because middle-class Americans have already signed on the dotted line, as we have already had occasion to note. What remains in place, stonelike, even as the assets shrink in value, is their *debt.* In a recession, borrowers' ability to service their debt burden is diminished, yet the monthly payments must still be made.

The parameters for Rented-For-Life have long been established; when it comes to making people jump through hoops in order to instill brand-name consciousness in them, modern marketers are peerless. Traditional advertising, which involved preaching the virtues of a product to target audiences sitting in front of radio and television sets, has been largely devalued; the new strategy involves engaging the populace in a frenzy of pin number punching, password submitting, prize-card scratching, and frequent-flyer mileage accumulating.

People are so exhausted by the ordeal of juggling all their cards and numbers and claiming their shopping "rewards," that they have no time to ask themselves what their existence has become—an ideal outcome, in the view of those who profit from the desires they discover in others.

22
Götterdämmerung

> Our principal views were the conservation of this power, great employments to ourselves, and great opportunities of rewarding those who had helped to raise us, and of hurting those who stood in opposition to us.
>
> —Henry St. John Bolingbroke

> He must fall and join the menial men.
> It was fraudulent counsel that he gave
> And ever since, I've been after his head.
>
> —Dante, *Divine Comedy*

The Media

By appealing to a taste for sensationalism, the financial cable channels left themselves vulnerable to changes in fashion—in effect, they sold out their audience, yet simultaneously outsmarted themselves by debasing their own currency, which was their credibility.

Many viewers were badly burned in the tech-stock crash, and they will not soon be returning to the markets—or to TV channels which lent hawkers of dubious financial vehicles so willing a platform. Because viewer ratings were a creature of the mania, they collapsed when it did.

Should it come as a surprise, that the lips of broadcast personalities weren't founts of pure objectivity? Perhaps those listening in should have used greater prudence. But that's what a mania does: It destroys the objectivity of those it infects.

The Venture Capitalists

Towards the end, VCs cranked out IPOs with the regularity of assembly lines. The IPO share allotment process, which was pure payola, demonstrated the extent to which the financial sector's share of the common spoils had grown at the expense of every other sector. By the time the underwriters had finished skimming their fees, and they had cut large clients in at the offering price, and the VCs had been set for life, and they had all finished marketing and advertising the whole thing to the public, and the public had paid the brokers their commissions and the mutual funds their management fees and the market makers their spreads, the average share of technology stock had been whittled down to the speculative equivalent of a lottery-ticket. Finance succeeded so well at muscling in on every other business activity, the entire nation eventually fell hostage to its extortion.

The VC money-machine became so fecund, it ground out more techno-clones than the market could absorb. The VC's worst nightmare—getting stuck with too many startups—had come to pass. Venture capital markets went into hibernation, and publicly-traded shares of prominent "incubator" stocks fell by more than 90 percent.

When one considers the arrogance of the VC kings in 1999, and examines them again a year or two later in their (relatively) humbled circumstances, it might seem like these financial gods have entered their twilight.

But then, venture capitalism goes in cycles, too.

The Dotcoms

From the fact that Internet companies were never designed to make money, it was inevitable that somebody was going to get stuck holding the bag. From the way margin debt spiked up right around New Year's Day 2000, it was obvious that the "somebody" in question was going to be the little guy.

Some of the riskiest investment vehicles were, in fact, little more than shell corporations—hollow entities that conformed to letter-of-the-law standards but had nothing to sell. Oh, they had a business plan, a board of directors, papers properly filed with the SEC, a web page, some computer engineers, and some computers. At the height of the frenzy on Wall Street, that was nearly enough to qualify for a billion-dollar capitalization.

As long as investment capital was poured into these companies with clockwork-like regularity, they "grew"; when realistic P/E criteria were applied, they looked terrible—it was a lucky thing that for the longest time nobody noticed.

Their revenue models were never realistic. They hired employees in a land-office rush and set them to work 80 hours a week on folding tables, but sadly, many of those workers ended the demoralizing experience with a handful of worthless stock options and an unceremoniously-delivered pink slip. The eagerness of Internet entrepreneurs to hire workers in 1999 was matched only by their ruthlessness in firing them one year later.

Many Internet startups failed at running a business—in this they hadn't a clue—but their founders still succeeded where it counted most: At maximizing their opportunities to exploit the middle class' insatiable appetite for high-priced stocks. A lot of company managers who never "managed" to achieve any of their growth or revenue goals still succeeded in exercising stock options worth millions.

The imperatives of capital had been satisfied, in spite of the broken dreams of countless workers who gave up steady jobs in 1999 to go "make a million" with an Internet startup.

The Investment Houses

In the wake of the investment community's colossal betrayal of its own clients, investors will need to ask themselves if their broker was their advisor—or their adversary. Because (forgive us!) some of the junk those brokers dropped on their clients (who, admittedly, were lining up begging to buy into IPOs) makes it look like the investor was their *dupe*.

Of course, in the course of bilking the retail investor, the investment houses, which hardly considered the damage that might do to their own interests, succeeded in debasing their own currency as well. A lucky thing for them that investor memories are so short!

Wall Street's tactics have long been designed to take advantage of this forgetfulness. The Quick Kill has been the anthem of Wall Street since its inception. Every epoch must have its philosophy, and the Age of the Quick Kill is no different. Its central tenet is the *sales pitch*.

As of May 2001, dozens of class-action suits had been filed against the big investment banks, seeking billions of dollars in damages for having allegedly rigged IPOs in the technology sector.[1]

The Corporate Insiders

After technology stocks had suffered their collapse, corporate insiders were cast as tragic characters who had had the world in their hands, only to let it slip away—"CEO Loses $1 Billion in One Day" stuff.

When the most successful tech visionaries made the rounds of cable TV news shows during the bubble's manic phase, they were invariably asked how it felt to be billionaires. Their answers reflected the same superficial modesty: Those gigantic gains existed "only on paper."

Funny how those CEOs wheeled out that same argument at the beginning of 2001—only this time it was to dispel the notion that something had really been lost in the market decline: The final price spike in the indexes had taken the market to truly stratospheric heights only briefly, so it didn't really matter that prices had fallen back since then.

What the CEOs didn't mention was how much money stuck to their fingers as it was trickling through.

The game was never about stock—silly you, you thought the stock market was about *stock?* No, it was always about *borrowing* based on the (inflated) price of stock, and then doing all kinds of neat stuff with the proceeds—wildly-inflated stock prices permitted wildly-out-of-control corporate spending.

Management convinced pet analysts to sign off on rosy earnings targets—not only for the next quarter, but for the next *five years*. We say "earnings," but these companies needed no earnings. They only needed a forecast showing that their *losses* would be reduced on a timetable.

Corporate insiders elucidated their giddy dreams at industry conferences, and, of course, they split their stocks often—in the bull market's heyday, a stock-split announcement provoked a "split run," a buying frenzy that drove the stock higher and higher before the rally finally petered out prior to the actual split date.

With a monstrous market cap and a few dozen balance sheet artists, these execs were ready to conquer the world.

Today, investors who can bring themselves to glance at their financial statements may well shrug their shoulders and credit the corporate insider who sold a couple of hundred million dollars of stock in his own company (just before that stock crashed) with nothing more than "getting lucky."

Suffice it to say that participation in the financial markets is Every Man For Himself.

23
What Goes Around . . .

Each of these relations leads to its opposite or to its own reversal, and does so by its own movement . . .

—Maurice Merleau-Ponty, *Adventures of the Dialectic*

Far from escaping comprehension, the deviations, errors, and setbacks are an integral part of it . . .

—Jean-Paul Sartre, *Second Critique*

We live in such extraordinary times, nobody needs history anymore—or so the story goes. These days, "staying in front of the curve" is said to be the only attribute one needs to attain fame and fortune.

"Is this the End of the Business Cycle?" asked delirious investors during the bubble. Had capitalism overcome its tendency towards bouts of manic depression?

But how could the business cycle be over, when 90 percent of the world's population couldn't afford any techno-toys, and the other 10 percent was already largely bored and sated by them?

History was tossed into the dustbin, but its lessons would eventually be repeated for the benefit of those who had been distracted for too long.

Early in the book, we suggested that Alan Greenspan's "virtuous cycle" was actually a vicious cycle. Saucer-eyed over the stratospheric returns others were nabbing, more and more investors jumped into the fray—so many, in fact, that eventually they poisoned the very markets they were hoping to exploit with their presence.

For years, recklessness, complacency, conspicuous greed, overspending, and ignorance were rewarded. Asset misallocation led to manufacturing overcapacity, which led to high inventory levels, which led to reduced returns on investment—and lower portfolio values.

In a mania, finance overwhelms the rest of the economy and goes on to cannibalize it. A boom—especially one sustained well past its "natural" death by an elaborate life support system—results in the *overproduction of investment products*.

Sooner or later, overly-fizzy economies go flat, and flat ones get stirred up again. A return to valuative normality is already implied at the beginning of a bubble; overvaluation is no more a permanent characteristic of the investment horizon than is undervaluation; both are cyclical in nature within capitalism and therefore repetitive.

The primary cause of investor inability to "read the future" isn't ineptitude at reading tea leaves or crystal balls—it is the failure to read the history of financial speculation. A period of lower-than-average returns *normally* follows a period of above-average returns. The failure to acknowledge this amounts to a failure to acknowledge that human beings live by cycles and rhythms.

24
Phenomenology of the Scam

> In the passage from fetish to symbol and from symbol to sign, value is gradually taken over by transcendence.
>
> —Jean-Joseph Goux, *Symbolic Economies*

After the fall of the Berlin Wall and the Soviet Union, advocates of "free enterprise" engaged in a veritable orgy of self-congratulation; a decade later they were laying considerably lower, hoping, perhaps, that nobody would notice that their global world economy had been strangely beset by some of the same problems which had once afflicted the Soviet Union.

In the heyday of state communism, senior Moscow bureaucrats wrote Five Year Plans dictating production quotas for everything from pig iron to butter. The system resulted in widespread inefficiency. Yet no matter how unrealistic the Soviet quota system, no matter how wasteful and useless the products it generated, it eventually met its match in the absurdities and excesses of the Age of the Dotcom, in which many of the companies brought to the market had about as much intrinsic value as a boxcar of extra-small Soviet shoes (left shoe only).

If the market is an almost infallible pricing mechanism in which all known or anticipated news is instantaneously discounted (as some economists insist), why did market participants *wait so long* before assigning Internet stocks values which more closely approximated their intrinsic worth?

Because of the way in which market economies operate, mispricing inevitably results in misallocation of natural and human resources. The market tends to misprice things rather frequently—the result of the powerful emotions which compete for primacy in the heads of otherwise "rational" investors.

Towards the end of the stock market price-riot, bull-boosters, in typical triumphal fashion, characterized the public's prodigious transfer of money into the hands of corporate insiders and VCs as a marvel of capitalist efficiency. They cited public willingness to sink billions into the "fastest growing sectors" of the American economy (i.e., into the pet projects of the top VCs) as the reason for the country's amazing "jump" on the rest of the world.

An alternative explanation is certainly possible: The money had been misallocated, and stock prices were too high. In 1999, a money-losing tech company could pull off a secondary stock offering and purchase the oil output of a minor gulf emirate with the proceeds—little surprise, then, that there were soon too many computer chips and too few barrels of crude oil on the market.

In the peculiar psychopathology which applied at the end of the last millennium, investors shunned companies that made money and drooled over those that lost it. "Brick and mortar" companies—that's the disparaging name they gave to traditional industries—were burdened with clunky physical infrastructures, creating inefficiencies which could be profitably exploited by web-based disintermediaries. These profitable but stodgy companies were complete dinosaurs, which, due to the bull-headedness of their directors, hadn't embraced the exciting "new paradigm" yet.

Besides, how could companies that made money match the allure, the *sexiness*, of a startup? In a superb contrarian indicator, Time Magazine named an online merchant its "Man of the Year" for 1999. The company hadn't made a penny's profit.

Did they forget to tell you all about the "new valuation matrices" which permitted the remorse-free purchase of stocks that had P/E ratios above 300? "Remember," they sagely counseled, "you're investing in the management team—not the earnings."

Fund managers and financial advisors preferred that investors not trouble themselves with arcane issues like overvaluation—these were for fund managers and financial advisors to worry about! They encouraged investors to look instead to the companies—the marvelous, magical companies, run by those evangelists of commerce, the *tech visionaries*. These consultant-groomed fairy tales had already been worked out on the IPO road-show circuit, and they were regurgitated whenever an investor needed to know why a particular stock was still a "buy" even after its P/E ratio had gone bonkers.

"Behind every stock in the fund is a great company," said the brochures. By the end of the mania the stock market had *become* the economy, so it was the stock and not the company that mattered.

When would these companies become profitable? In the case of many of them: Never. For those who bought in near the top, the fabled "information superhighway" turned into a road to financial pauperdom.

This journey to ruin for many may be compared to the Klondike and other fabled gold rushes of years past. Towns that were built to last one hundred years became ghost towns after five; so, too, at the beginning of the twenty-first century, Silicon Valley dreams comically overshot the mark.

Starry-eyed investors certainly failed to exhibit reasonable caution during the last stages of the rally, but we must look deeper than that if we are to understand why Internet stocks became so overvalued. We must ask ourselves: *How was such pervasive overvaluation even possible?*

25
Opacity

He carried me off to Minos, who twisted
His tail eight times around his unbending back
And bit it in a fit of rage.

—Dante, *Divine Comedy*

The market makes the traders as much as the traders make the market; they internalize its dictates even as they constitute it.

In the financial marketplace, participants act together, but *not in unison*. Bulls and bears are like "two contending subgroups" which, "in a kind of negative collaboration, produce a common '*antilabor*' originally intended by neither . . ."[1] Market players are never quite united, because market makers always impose a "spread" between them.

Participants don't trust those they trade with enough to enter into transactions with them without the intermediation of a third party, which indemnifies each against the potential default of the other. The regulated exchanges are nothing but rubrics under which widely separated counterparties are temporarily united and then relieved of any further responsibilities to one another. That parties submit their association to mediation in spite of the costs entailed in granting a third party this power, says much about the strained circumstances of their "union."

The mediation, which is performed by the financial exchanges in consort with licensed brokers, dealers, and government and industry regulators, doesn't actually increase the level of trust between participants; if it did, traders could disintermediate the middlemen and pay no fees or commissions of any kind to execute their mutual transactions.

Mediators make it possible for counterparties to have a relationship in *spite* of the mutual distrust they feel for each other. But they cannot make that distrust disappear.

"The individuals are physically close to each other but they remain a collection of solitary people. They have nothing in common save an intention that unites and opposes them."[2]

Opacity—the inability of investors to consistently "peg" the market and its tendency to consistently confound them—is the most significant characteristic of the need for mediation.

The market is a thing both human and inhuman, that is to say, it is a social creature. The numbers flashing on trading screens all around the world are in some sense actually alive, as objectifications of the blood, sweat, and tears of millions of individual traders and investors. Yet they are "just" numbers.

Insofar as the market tends to deviate from the expectations and aims of many—if not most—of its participants, it is perverse. Thus do traders sometimes speak of the market in almost mystical terms, as a creature that makes all those on the wrong side of any trade suffer the maximum pain before exiting the position.

26
The Void

> To this Court, an empty mirage consumed in designating an absence . . . comes the artist to nourish his profound conviction that nothing is beautiful save that which does not exist.
>
> —Jean-Paul Sartre, *The Family Idiot*

In 1971, the Nixon administration made the U.S. dollar inconvertible to gold. Today, if the greenback is no longer backed by anything real, what makes it worth something?

According to state officials (who are perhaps not the best ones to ask), a government decree, or *fiat,* makes a nation's paper money worth something. That is sheer nonsense, of course; paper money is intrinsically quite worthless, except when it is collected in large bundles and burnt for warmth.

In the "history of the money function," theorist Jean-Joseph Goux discerns "a movement towards idealization"[1] passing from fetish to trinket to electronic trace. "In place of products with material value, increasingly abstract monetary signs are gradually substituted."[2]

In the process, matter and value are "split."[3] Once this happens, the potential for overvaluation is unlimited. As soon as idealized value has been substituted for real worth, the ideological preconditions for a speculative bubble have been met.

The danger for abuse lies in the fact that money, insofar as it *represents* value, *stands in for* and in effect *replaces* that value. According to the logic of substitution, "gold can be replaced by worthless symbols of itself . . ."[4]

As the level of symbolization increases, so does the risk for assets' prices to become more and more detached from their values. Once this happens, appreciation in asset prices doesn't enhance *value*.

Between 1984 and 1999, the United States experienced severe asset inflation, even as the prices of consumer goods stayed in a long-term disinflationary trend. Towards the end, it became exceedingly expensive to participate in "growth." Through the simple act of bidding stocks up, cash itself had been rather badly discounted.

Think of it as an act of collective indulgence.

When (taken by the excitement of the times) Americans chased the most speculative stocks, their actions corresponded to an increasing idealization of the value-function. With all the enthusiasm for "virtual" anything, it isn't surprising that stock market valuations got "virtual," too.[5]

But the extent of fantasy, like the price of stock, is itself cyclical in nature. In bull markets, investors forget the value of simply having their principal returned to them; but when they feel the claws of the bear, they are given ample cause to recall it. One day they may even share John Locke's insight, that "the natural worth of anything consists in its fitness to supply the necessities, or serve the conveniences of human life."[6]

27
Complicit Victims

The very basis of the bullfight depends on the fact that the bulls must learn about men *after* they are in the ring. If they are tampered with on the range, or even worked too much in the tests, they will remember, add to their knowledge, and prove dangerous and almost unkillable in the ring.

—Homer Casteel, Jr., *Running of the Bulls*

He is in Hell because he relied *absolutely* on the 'counsel' of his 'mediator.' He *ought* to have had better 'insight' (and the 'courage to use it').

—H.S. Harris, *Hegel's Ladder*

Since the Vietnam War, working Americans have been financially screwed at least once every decade—by the inflation of the 1970s; the leveraged buyout predation, real-estate busts, and S&L fiascos of the 1980s; and the Internet rip-offs of the 1990s. The crashes and liquidations were indicative of a shift in investor preferences—and were fresh proof that golden mirages can't pay off for everyone.

Get Yours While You Can—hardly an edifying credo by which to live your life.

The overpricing of tech stocks in 1999 must be understood as a single instance of a much larger phenomenon: America's pervasive overvaluation of economic growth.

Everything investors assumed was true—the Articles of Bullish Faith, ranging from the virtuousness of dollar-cost averaging to the end of the business cycle—turned out to be true only of specific bull market periods, not universally.

While a few select scapegoats will end up fielding the blame, the Great Bull Market of the 1990s will likely be remembered as one of those collective acts of greed and robbery that are simply too big to properly redress. For those who lost money, the realization of their own fantastic gullibility is only now beginning to dawn.

The dismal fate endured by Nasdaq investors in the year 2000 illustrates the fallacy of "long-term investing." The stock market can and does go up for 10 or even 15 years; but it can't go up forever. Contrary to public opinion, the market isn't a magical means for conjuring wealth out of thin air.

Stumbling into the new millennium, the American middle class exhibited no more consciousness of the fact that its stock-buying binges had been grossly excessive, than had the residents of Amsterdam at the height of their tulip-buying craze several hundred years earlier. Those who bought tech stocks in 1999 and thought they were investing in real companies were largely deluding themselves—what they were actually doing was fueling the last stage of *somebody else's* Ponzi scheme.

What permitted the flawed paradigm of permanent bullishness to go uncorrected for so long?

On the one side stood the Boys, cold professionals who enjoyed a considerable informational advantage over "Mom n' Pop" investors. Those pros knew how to evaluate risk and mitigate it in the global marketplace, 24 hours a day—they knew how to *cut their losses*.

On the other side were small investors, many of whom knew little or nothing about the financial instruments in which they were investing. After a long bull market, they lacked a thorough understanding of the systemic risks to which they had so enthusiastically exposed themselves. And they were psychologically committed to remaining invested, no matter what.

It was never a fair game. *But who ever said it was?*

Middle-class investors are learning that those who pitch the philosophy of eternal bullishness do not always embrace it—and that uninformed market participants are *ripe pickings* for those who know that bubbles don't last. The pockets of middle-class investors have been repeatedly picked, but the middle class has been complicit in its own victimization. Until people break out of their exhausted apathy, more periodic bilking is to be expected.

28
Are We Having Fun Yet?

> The gap grows between the intensity of experience and that of its manifestations; he cannot help feeling an emotional inflation—not much gold, lots of paper money.
>
> —Jean-Paul Sartre, *The Family Idiot*

If Americans bought stocks early in the great bull market and sold them at or near the top, they did extremely well for themselves. Those who didn't play the market—half the population—were almost certainly *worse* off, however, because they found themselves in an increasingly *unaffordable* America. The bull-boosters conveniently ignored that—so what if a minimum-wage worker had to work for six theoretical lifetimes to pay off a house? In their view, the engine of growth was capital; cheap labor was merely an additional boon.

If the costs for market excesses, which must always be paid in full by the little folks, were instead borne equally by all, one could almost overlook the fact that benefits haven't been shared equally. As it turns out, many of those who profited inequitably on the up leg also made a pile on the down leg.

As bullish investors stubbornly bore the brunt of the fall in stock prices, investment banks and VCs had already booked massive profits by delivering themselves from many of the momentum stocks that would soon crash.

There's no reason for hot money to remain in a single underperforming asset one millisecond after an asset manager has determined that money can fetch a better return elsewhere. And when big money leaves, it leaves factory towns, currencies—and the populations of entire nations—destitute.[1]

The popular perception that investment analysts, CEOs, and media pundits are "objective" amounts to an investiture of public trust in these figures. But then, for those who profit from the greed and fear they find in others, public trust is always just one more currency worth debasing as thoroughly as possible.

29
Definite Disarray

> History offers no lack of examples [of panic], from the Great Fear of the year 1000 to that of the summer of 1789, from the stock market crashes of the nineteenth century through the atomic panics touched off by radio programs to, finally, the diffuse panic we live in, precipitated by ill-advised acts that are the fruits of disarray . . .
>
> —Louis Althusser, *Specter of Hegel*

What about the other costs of the great "economic miracle"? What about the workaholic families, the load of stress, the busted marriages, the soulless suburban *cul-de-sacs*, and the deadly grind of taxes and commuting?

Deeper yet are the psychological costs. Simply to "succeed," young people must adopt a ruthless marketplace mentality when they take a job—a minor psychological calamity too often confused with "maturity." It is something for which young people are often woefully unprepared, in spite of all the "education" they receive. The workplace manages to get under their skin, often at the cost of the deformation of their personalities, and it never adequately compensates them for this. Whether it be through the forced toleration of a nasty boss or the telling of tiny lies to customers in order to keep an account, these compromises do have their psychological cost. Oh sure, maybe workers end up with a nice house and a couple of cars, but they are so busy servicing the corresponding debt that they have little or no time to enjoy their possessions.

The lesson of this latest mania isn't only that many people paid much too much for their stock—if it was, shrugging off a bunch of bad losers would fix it. Misallocation of funds is symptomatic of a more fundamental misallocation: Of subjectivity in favor of objectification; of human growth in favor of economic growth; of human scale in favor of industrial gigantism; and of life in favor of things.

All that glitters isn't gold . . .

Notes

Chapter One: Fireworks

1. Chairman Greenspan, *Testimony Before the Joint Economic Committee, U.S. Congress*, 9 June 1998.

2. That is to say, moral hazard not only existed, but flourished.

Chapter Three: Don't Look Now

1. The ills of the rest of the world economy also indicated the extent to which things had become unbalanced: Mexico and Japan were slipping into recession; Southeast Asia had become a glutted inventory warehouse for technology gadgets after suffering the twin slings of a collapsed bubble—which had been caused by foreign investment—and the collapse of overvalued Asian currencies.

Chapter Six: Uh-Oh

The opening quotation is by L.E. Willoughby, Kansas State Agricultural College official, during the Great Depression, cited in Worster, *Dust Bowl*, 139.

Chapter Eight: The Provocation

1. "Thus there has been history, but there is no longer any." Marx, *Poverty of Philosophy*, 174.

2. A single investment house can underwrite an initial public offering (IPO), make bullish recommendations on that stock to clients through its brokerage wing, collect commissions as its clients enter positions in that stock, and then—this is really the sweetest part—sell the same stock *short* through its proprietary trading arm.

3. Yet traders like George Soros consistently achieved returns far in excess of the market benchmarks.

4. Even for those who believe this, it does not follow that staying eternally invested is a good idea; one can trade in and out of the market, while remaining invested during times when the "odds"—as determined from technical indicators and market sentiment numbers—favor rising equity prices.

Chapter Nine: To the Rescue

1. Chairman Greenspan, *Testimony Before the Committee on Banking and Financial Services, U.S. House of Representatives*, 1 October 1998, www.federalreserve.gov. All subsequent quotations by the chairman on the topic of LTCM in the present chapter are taken from this source.

2. Conover, Todd, *Testimony at Hearings Before the Subcommittee on Financial Institutions, Supervision, Regulation, and Insurance*, Sept./Oct. 1984, 287-8.

3. Those charged with regulating the economy ought to adequately stress-test it. These days the Federal Reserve conducts stress-tests, but their worst-case assumptions are laughably tame, i.e., in the range of only two to three standard deviations. The very nature of a high standard deviation event is that almost nobody expects it.

4. The chairman did note that "LTCM's embrace of risk on a large scale produced stunning losses," and he even went so far as to describe the busted hedge fund's habit of "employing more leverage and increasing its exposure to risk" as "a strategy that was destined to fail." The fatalism of the chairman's testimony came as a startling contrast to the omnipotence with which he is usually credited.

5. Dunbar, *Inventing Money*, 158-9.

6. In any case, when compared to the lifestyles of 90 percent of the world's population, American "austerity" seems like luxury.

Chapter Ten: Hyperactivity in High Places

1. At any given moment, there are enormous repositories of loot, billions—if not trillions—of dollars, just there for the plundering. If stocks had already fully priced in potential earnings for years ahead, where did the best chance for profiting from equity market volatility lie? Clearly, if stocks could scarcely rise any further above their already-absurd valuations, there was only one way to make money in the markets: Go short. At the beginning of 2000, market valuations represented a huge pot of gold, and smart players resolved to have at it.

Taken as a whole, the Boys' size does them in when they try to play the short end too aggressively. While they can (and sometimes do) run fantastically profitable short positions during bear markets—their unabashed boosterism of the bull notwithstanding—the Boys stand to make much more packaging and piggybacking securities than they do on the short end. Oh, they will short without the slightest compunction, especially for hedging purposes, even in stocks they are simultaneously touting on the long side to investors, but the short-seller's universe is much smaller than the world of mutual funds and 401Ks, which yield lucky asset managers a couple of percent a year—for perpetuity.

Chapter Twelve: Great White Sharks

1. *R.A. Holdman & Co. v. SEC*, 366 F2d 446 449 (2d Cir 1966).

Chapter Fourteen: The Sound of **it Hitting the Fan

1. If the most rabid market enthusiasts have their way, Social Security money—the ultimate treasure-chest—will be poured into the market as well.

Chapter Fifteen: The Same Boat?

1. The Reagan team succeeded so well at implementing a regimen of economic rationalization that by 1987 there was, once again, a stock market bubble in need of popping.

Chapter Seventeen: Gas and a Burger, Please

1. As reported by Bloomberg.com on 2 March 2001.

2. "Within the field of a universal Lie the 'repressed' truth will emerge in the guise of a particular contingent event . . ." Žižek, *Plague of Fantasies*, 127.

Chapter Twenty: Trickle Where?

1. Wessel, David, *Wall Street Journal*, 15 March 1999, quoted in www.sharedcapitalism.org/scfacts.html.

2. Henwood, Doug, *The Nation*, 19 July 1999, quoted in www.sharedcapitalism.org/scfacts.html.

3. *Federal Reserve Bulletin*, January 2000, quoted in www.sharedcapitalism.org/scfacts.html.

4. As reported at http://www.federalreserve.gov/pubs/bulletin/2000/0700lead.pdf

5. These bonds are directly or indirectly linked to every other bond since all are priced in relation to benchmark, "risk-free," U.S. Government bonds of comparable duration.

6. Structured investment strategies include, for example, the dividing of an asset into layers, called *tranches*. At the height of the tranche madness, in "the early 1990s, mortgage pools were being routinely cut up into 60 different CMO tranches, often with three or four classes of Z-bonds at the bottom of the structure and a wild profusion of floaters, strips, Companions, sticky-jump Zs—a whole new race of financial gargoyles." Morris, *Money, Greed, and Risk*, 200.

Chapter Twenty-One: Hardcore Junkie

1. Chairman Greenspan, *Testimony Before the Committee on Banking and Financial Services, U.S. House of Representatives*, 1 October 1998, www.federalreserve.gov.

2. The Boys were too smart to just sit on all that risk, especially so late in the economic cycle, so they sloughed it off by selling bundles of fast-degrading receivables in the ABS market.

Chapter Twenty-Two: Götterdämmerung

The opening quotation is by Henry St. John Bollingbroke, *A Letter to Sir William Windham* (1753), cited in De Jouvenel, *On Power*, 126.

1. As reported by *The Times [of London]* on 29 May 2001.

Chapter Twenty-Five: Opacity

1. Aronson, *Sartre's Second Critique*, 102, and citing Jean-Paul Sartre, *Second Critique*, in a different context.

2. Aron, *Dialectic of Violence*, 54, in a different context.

Chapter Twenty-Six: The Void

1. Goux, *Symbolic Economies*, 50-51.

2. Ibid., 49. We consider this process cyclical rather than progressive.

3. Ibid.

4. Ibid., 47, citing Marx.

5. If absolute returns are the goal and risk is not a concern, the best approach is to "strip" a stock or a bond or a currency of its "body," and give it a Pure Body that is pure volatility. In this way, financial leverage is

increased, and all material limitations to the accumulation of wealth fade to unimportance. This search for a pure investment vehicle unadorned with the "weight" that slows down the underlying instruments leads to the pursuit and embrace of pure volatility, of volatility for volatility's sake. Therefore it makes sense that the most aggressive market players trade derivatives rather than the underlying instruments. Also see Paul Virilio's *Speed and Politics*.

6. Cited in Marx and Engels, *Collected Works*, 35:46.

Chapter Twenty-Eight: Are We Having Fun Yet?

1. Hedge funds which short emerging market currencies usually don't cover their bets until the target cries "uncle"!

Bibliography

Adorno, Theodor. *Negative Dialectics*. New York: The Continuum Publishing Company, 1995.

Althusser, Louis. *The spectre of Hegel: Early writings*. Translated by G.M. Goshgarian. New York: Verso, 1997.

Aron, Raymond. *History and the Dialectic of Violence*. Translated by Barry Cooper. New York: Harper & Row, 1975.

Aronson, Ronald. *Sartre's Second Critique*. Chicago: University of Chicago Press, 1987.

Balibar, Etienne. *The Philosophy of Marx*. Translated by Chris Turner. New York: Verso, 1995.

Barnes, Hazel E. *Sartre and Flaubert*. Chicago: University of Chicago Press, 1981.

Bataille, Georges. *The Accursed Share*. Translated by Robert Hurley. 3 vols. Zone Books, 1991-3.

Benjamin, Walter. *Selected Writings: 1913-1926*. Cambridge, Mass.: Harvard University Press, Belknap Press, 1996.

Borch-Jacobsen, Mikkel. *Lacan: The Absolute Master*. Translated by Douglas Brick. Stanford: Stanford University, 1991.

Buck-Morss, Susan. *The Dialectics of Seeing: Walter Benjamin and the Arcades Project*. 2d ed. Cambridge, Mass.: MIT Press, 1995.

Casteel, Jr., Homer. *The Running of the Bulls*. New York: Dodd, Mead and Company, 1953.

De Jouvenel, Bertrand. *On Power: The Natural History of Its Growth*. Translated by J.F. Huntington. Indianapolis: Liberty Fund, 1993.

Derrida, Jacques. *A Derrida Reader*. Edited by Peggy Kamuf. New York: Columbia University Press, 1991.

Dunbar, Nicholas. *Inventing Money: The Story of Long-Term Capital Management and the Legends Behind It*. West Sussex: John Wiley & Sons Ltd., 2000.

Eagleton, Terry. *Ideology: An Introduction*. New York: Verso, 1991.

Feuerbach, Ludwig. *The Essence of Christianity*. Translated by George Eliot. Buffalo, N.Y.: Prometheus Books, 1989.

Foucault, Michel. *Birth of the Clinic*.Translated by A.M. Sheridan Smith. New York: Vintage Books, 1994.

Goldman, Robert, and Stephen Papson. *Sign Wars: The Cluttered Landscape of Advertising*. New York: Guilford Press, 1996.

Goux, Jean-Joseph. *Symbolic Economies: After Marx and Freud*. Translated by Jennifer Curtiss Gage. Ithaca, N.Y.: Cornell University Press, 1990.

Harris, H.S. *Hegel's Ladder II: The Odyssey of Spirit*. Indianapolis: Hackett, 1997.

Hill, Geoffrey. *Collected Poems*. New York: Oxford University Press, 1986.

Kafka, Franz. *Collected Stories*. New York: Alfred Knopf, Everyman's Library, 1993.

Larsen, Sein Ugelvik. *Who Were the Fascists: Social Roots of European Fascism*. Olso: Universitetsforlaget, 1980.

Luttwak, Edward. *Turbo-Capitalism: Winners and Losers in the Global Economy*. New York: HarperCollins, 2000.

Marx, Karl, and Frederick Engels. *Collected Works*. 37 vols. New York: New York International publishers, 1996.

Merleau-Ponty, Maurice. *Adventures of the Dialectic*. Translated by Joseph Bien. 2d ed. Evanston, IL: Northwestern University Press, 1995.

———. *The Visible and the Invisible*. Translated by Alphonso Lingis. Evanston: Northwestern University Press, 1968.

Morris, Charles R. *Money, Greed, and Risk: Why Financial Crises and Crashes Happen*. New York: Random House, Times Books, 1999.

Nietzsche, Friedrich. *The Portable Nietzsche*. Edited and translated by Walter Kaufmann. New York: Penguin Books, 1954.

Perlman, Fredy. *Against His-story, Against Leviathan!* Detroit: Black & Red, 1983.

Pines, Christopher L. *Ideology and False Consciousness: Marx and His Historical Progenitors*. Albany, N.Y.: SUNY Press, 1993.

Sartre, Jean-Paul. *The Family Idiot: Gustave Flaubert*. Translated by Carol Cosman. 5 vols. Chicago: University of Chicago Press, 1993.

———. *Critique of Dialectical Reason*. Translated by Quintin Hoare. New York: Verso, 1991.

Searle, John R. *The Construction of Social Reality*. New York: Simon and Schuster, Free Press, 1995.

Virilio, Paul. *Speed and Politics*. Translated by Mark Polizzoti. New York: Semiotexte, 1986.

Virno, Paolo, and Michael Hardt, eds. *Radical Thought in Italy: A Potential Politics*. Minneapolis: University of Minnesota, 1996.

Worster, Donald. *Dust Bowl: The Southern Plains in the 1930s*. Oxford: Oxford University Press, 1979.

Žižek, Slavoj. *The Plague of Fantasies*. New York: Verso, 1997.

———. *For They Know Not What They Do: Enjoyment as a Political Factor.* New York: Verso, 1991.

The source of all Dante quotations in *Bleeding Bull* is the *Divine Comedy*, *Inferno*, *Canto XXVII*, wherein Guido da Montefeltro tells how he was corrupted into giving false counsel, and fell to the Eighth Circle of hell.

Translated and abridged by Vladimir Sarkoff.